Liquidity Preference and Monetary Economies

The 2008 international crisis has revived the interest in Keynes's theories and, in particular, on Minsky's models of financial fragility. The core proposition of these theories is that money plays an essential role in modern economies, which is usually neglected in other approaches. This is Keynes's liquidity preference theory, which is also the foundation for Minsky's model, a theory that had been largely forgotten in recent years.

This book looks at liquidity preference theory and its most important problems, showing how one should understand the role of money in modern monetary economies. It develops Keynes's and Minsky's *financial* view of money, relating it to the process of capital accumulation, the determination of effective demand and the theory of output, and employment as a whole.

Building on the author's significant body of work in the field, this book delves into a broad range of topics allowing the general reader to understand propositions that have been mistreated in the literature including Keynes and the concept of monetary production economy; uncertainty, expectations and money; short and long period; liquidity preference theory as a theory of asset pricing under uncertainty; asset prices and capital accumulation; Keynes's version of the principle of effective demand; and the role of macroeconomic policy. It will be essential reading for all students and scholars of Post-Keynesian economics.

Fernando J. Cardim de Carvalho is Emeritus Professor at the Federal University of Rio de Janeiro, Brazil.

Routledge Critical Studies in Finance and Stability
Edited by Jan Toporowski
School of Oriental and African Studies, University of London, UK

The 2007–2008 Banking Crash has induced a major and wide-ranging discussion on the subject of financial (in)stability and a need to revaluate theory and policy. The response of policy-makers to the crisis has been to refocus fiscal and monetary policy on financial stabilisation and reconstruction. However, this has been done with only vague ideas of bank recapitalisation and 'Keynesian' reflation aroused by the exigencies of the crisis, rather than the application of any systematic theory or theories of financial instability.

Routledge Critical Studies in Finance and Stability covers a range of issues in the area of finance including instability, systemic failure, financial macroeconomics in the vein of Hyman P. Minsky, Ben Bernanke and Mark Gertler, central bank operations, financial regulation, developing countries and financial crises, new portfolio theory and New International Monetary and Financial Architecture.

Liquidity Preference and Monetary Economies

Fernando J. Cardim de Carvalho

Routledge
Taylor & Francis Group

LONDON AND NEW YORK

First published 2015 by Routledge

2 Park Square, Milton Park, Abingdon, Oxfordshire OX14 4RN
52 Vanderbilt Avenue, New York, NY 10017

Routledge is an imprint of the Taylor & Francis Group, an informa business

First issued in paperback 2020

British Library Cataloguing in Publication Data
A catalogue record for this book is available from the British Library

Library of Congress Cataloging in Publication Data
Carvalho, Fernando J. Cardim de,
Liquidity preference and monetary economies /
Fernando J. Cardim de Carvalho.
    pages cm
    1. Liquidity (Economics) 2. Money. 3. Monetary policy.
    4. Keynesian economics. I. Title.
    HG178.C37 2015
    339.5'3–dc23   2014047184

ISBN: 978-1-138-83838-3 (hbk)
ISBN: 978-0-367-59911-9 (pbk)

Typeset in Times New Roman
by Wearset Ltd, Boldon, Tyne and Wear

To Carolina and Daniel

Contents

Acknowledgments

The ideas contained in this book, besides their obvious inspiration in Keynes's own writings, owe a lot to discussions, conversations and joint work with a large number of people. I can't possibly thank them all in this space, so I hope I may be forgiven to name only a few. Jan Kregel, Julio Lopez and Gary Dymski, besides being close friends, have always been ready to share their views and to enlighten me both on points of theory and of empirical realities. Jan has also accepted my invitation to write the foreword to this volume which, I am sure, will enhance whatever value it may have to readers. Among my Brazilian fellow Keynesians, working with the Money and Finance Study Group (MFSG) in the Institute of Economics of the Federal University of Rio de Janeiro, my place of employment, has been of decisive importance in my intellectual formation since the mid-1990s. I have been lucky enough to have had in my academic career the most pleasurable experience of seeing some of my former students becoming my colleagues, many of them as participants in the MFSG. I will mention only my closest associate, Jennifer Hermann, and the youngest member, Andre Modenesi, to represent the whole group. I have also to mention a few colleagues with which we founded the Brazilian Keynesian Association which has served as an important means of making Keynesian ideas and policies known in my country, Fernando Ferrari Filho, Luiz Fernando de Paula and José Luís Oreiro, the presidents that Association has had so far.

I must also express my gratitude to Francisco Eduardo Pires de Souza, with whom I co-wrote several papers on the Brazilian economy. A "pure" economist of Keynesian affiliation is practically an oxymoron. One central legacy of Keynes, the economist, the intellectual and the individual is certainly the notion that economics is either an instrument to understand the real world or is just a sterile and useless exercise. As could not be otherwise, the Brazilian economy has been at the center of my personal interests, and working with Pires de Souza has allowed me to learn a great deal about my own country.

As I observed in a book I published more than twenty years ago, my debts towards my two mentors, the late Antonio Barros de Castro and Paul Davidson, are still outstanding and I very much doubt I will ever be able to repay it.

For more than thirty years, all my research work has been unfailingly financially supported by the National Research Council of Brazil (CNPq), to which I want to express my deep gratitude.

I want to express my gratitude to Professor Jan Toporowski for taking the initiative of suggesting my name to Routledge to take part in the collection of which he is the editor. I also want to thank the Routledge who have prepared this edition.

Finally, I have to thank Fernanda, my wife. She pushed me toward an academic career when I was hesitant almost forty years ago and we have shared the pleasures and difficulties of it ever since. She had been encouraging me to write a book in recent years. I hope she will be satisfied with the result.

* * *

I must express my thanks to the publishers below for their permission to reprint the following papers in this volume:

Oxford University Press, for the permission to reprint "Uncertainty and money: Keynes, Tobin and Kahn and the disappearance of the precautionary demand for money from liquidity preference theory," originally published in the *Cambridge Journal of Economics*, 34 (4), 709–725, 2010.

Oxford University Press, for the permission to reprint "Liquidity preference of banks and crises," originally published in the volume *Keynesian Reflections*, edited by C. Marcuzzo, P. Mehrling and T. Hirai, 2013, 149–171.

Edward Elgar, for the permission to reprint "Keynes and the endogeneity of money," originally published in the *Review of Keynesian Economics*, 1 (4), 431–446, Winter, 2013.

Edward Elgar, for the permission to reprint "Aggregate savings, finance and investment," originally published in *Intervention. European Journal of Economics and Economic Policies*, 9 (2), 197–213, 2012.

Metropolis Verlag, for the permission to reprint "Systemic crisis, systemic risk and the financial instability hypothesis," originally published in the volume *Macroeconomic Policies on Shaky Foundations*, edited by E. Hein, T. Niechoj and E. Hammer, 2009, 261–282.

Centro de Economia Política, for the permission to reprint "Economic policies for monetary economies," originally published in *Revista de Economia Política*, 17 (4), 31–51, October/November, 1997.

I also want to thank Cambridge University Press for the permission to quote from *The Collected Writings of John Maynard Keynes*, 30 volumes, edited by Donald Moggridge and Elizabeth Johnson, published by Cambridge University Press for The Royal Economic Society, 2012–2013.

Foreword

Jan Kregel

The Great Depression of the 1930s was a defining moment in economic theory and economic policy. When orthodox policies did not work, something else had to be proposed. The result was the "New Deal" in the United States, and the elaboration of Keynesian demand management. After the interruption of World War II, a period of sustained expansion that was called a "golden age" in the 1960s followed by a "great moderation" in the 1980s and 1990s led many economists to believe that they had discovered the policy tools necessary to manage stable expansion of the economy over time. The events of 2007–2008 and the continuing Great Recession have not confirmed those beliefs. Unfortunately, this has produced little critical reflection. Indeed, even those who expected a return to, or at least a review of, the policies applied with success in the 1930s have been disappointed.

What went wrong? There has been a plethora of books and articles trying to explain just exactly what went wrong, covering every conceivable explanation from financial fraud and deception to excessive government interference or incompetence to unpredictable 100-year floods. But hardly any economists have been willing to shoulder blame for having based the economic policies of the golden age or the great moderation on lacunae in economic theory. And the same has been true of the failure of the economy to recovery rapidly to the energetic central bank policy response to the crisis.

This book demonstrates that the answer is to be found in the misunderstanding of the essence of the theory that Keynes proposed in response to the Great Depression. It was this misunderstanding that produced the conditions that eventually led to another crisis, a crisis which many thought impossible. But even more importantly, this misunderstanding has made it impossible to understand and respond to the current Depression. Part of the problem is that these misunderstandings are to be found in both critics and supporters of Keynes's theory. Today Keynesian economics is encapsulated in the idea of deficit spending and the investment multiplier. But there is virtually no detailed discussion of the former in Keynes's book, and the latter was originally developed by Richard Kahn long before Keynes's book was finished. Cardim de Carvalho shows clearly that these were not the innovative elements in Keynes's analysis, noting that most of Keynes's recommendations on fiscal policy date from the post-war reconstruction period and have been largely ignored by the profession.

Cardim de Carvalho is not an uncritical student of Keynes, and he notes that a large part of the problem is to be found in Keynes's own presentation of his new approach in the General Theory and subsequent attempts at clarification. Cardim de Carvalho provides a meticulous dissection of the ambiguities and deviations from the central message of the original book. His approach is based on the financial or monetary Keynesianism of Minsky and Davidson, and it should not be surprising that these criticisms are primarily in the area of the relation between money, finance and effective demand, and in particular the absent analysis of detailed discussions in the General Theory of the operation of banks and the financial system. A similar absence has been noted in the forecasting models used by the major central banks in assessing the impact of their policies on the economic system. The book provides a comprehensive presentation of Keynes's work on these issues in his other writings, which Cardim de Carvalho suggests might have more usefully been included in the 1936 book.

The title reflects Keynes's own assessment of the key element in his new approach: the concept of liquidity preference. While orthodox and traditional Keynesian authors consider this as a theory of the demand for money to replace the Quantity equation or the Marshallian version of the stable demand for money function that buttressed the monetarist counter-revolution, Cardim de Carvalho argues that the concept was instead meant to serve as a theory of asset prices.

And here we discover the importance of the concept for the current crisis, which is largely believed to have been caused by a distortion in asset prices, and whose solution is sought in an attempt by central banks to influence asset prices. While the monetarist approach through the quantity theory emphasizes the impact of the money supply on goods prices, it has virtually nothing to say about the determination of asset prices. But this is precisely where Keynes's theory starts in noting that liquidity preference will have its primary influence on asset prices and interest rates, and then in conjunction with the marginal efficiency of capital on investment final demand through the multiplier. A proper understanding of the causes of the crisis, and why the policies currently being implemented have had such limited success comes only with an understanding of liquidity reference.

Cardim de Carvalho stresses that while the traditional demand for money is at best linked to the current level of activity, liquidity preference is based on expectations of future conditions made necessary by the fact that current portfolio decisions will have an impact on future decisions that cannot be made with certainty – the basic reason for money to be held as an asset in portfolios to satisfy liquidity preference.

In the General Theory Keynes limited his discussion to the portfolio decisions of households, but liquidity preference is clearly relevant to banks' portfolio decisions, that is to the decisions to lend against real activity or against the purchase of financial assets and thus to the transmission mechanism between the central bank's balance sheet and the creation of credit to finance expenditure.

One of the most perplexing aspects of Fed policy in the 1930s and in the response to the current crisis has been the failure of expansion of the central bank's balance sheet, the creation of High powered money in monetarist parlance, to produce any increase in the money supply or the financing of expenditure. The basic objective of the rescue of the financial system and the policies of zero interest rates and quantitative easing have been to maintain lending to the private sector to support output and employment. Yet, the money supply growth has been non-existent, and the money multiplier moribund. In contrast to the traditional metaphor of the unthirsty horse being led to water that it refuses to drink, in this approach the problem may not be the lack of thirst, but rather the unwillingness of the banks to provide the water. If banks are unwilling to undertake the risks of lending to the private sector because they prefer to hold risk-free reserves at the central bank earning twenty-five basis points, this is a representation of the preference to remain liquid rather than extend credit. Indeed, Cardim de Carvalho notes that even Friedman and Schwartz's explanation of the lack of expansion of the money supply in the Great Depression relies on the explicit mention of the "liquidity preference" of banks impacting their balance sheets.

The book thus serves not only as a guide to Keynes for those who have had difficulty understanding his central message and importance in highlighting the role of money in determining economic activity, it also provides a guide to understanding why current policies have been so slow in bringing the economy back to recovery.

1 Introduction

Liquidity preference in monetary economies

In 1933, halfway between the publication of *A Treatise on Money* and *The General Theory of Employment, Interest and Money* (hereafter the GT), Keynes announced that he was working on a new conceptual framework to describe the dynamics of modern economies. He confessed to be dissatisfied with the way some essential problems were treated by the theories that were dominant at the time (and still are) and despaired of the possibility of reforming them. He reckoned that progress could only be made if those theories were replaced.

Experienced practitioners of any academic discipline know how difficult and painful such an endeavor is. Contrary to what is sometimes assumed, realism alone is not a sufficient reason to propose new fundamental concepts the content of which will be foreign to other practitioners. One has to face misunderstandings and the resistance of other practitioners whose careers were built relying on the development of established ideas, both solid obstacles to conceptual revolutions in any field. Many would-be revolutionaries are aware of how time- and effort- consuming persuading academic colleagues may be and, worst of all, that all the effort may end up being in vain.

The practical value of realism itself can be difficult to ascertain anyway. Fully realistic models, after all, can be impossibly complex to handle while simplistic renditions of a given situation may sometimes yield some valuable insights. The dilemma may be even worse for people like Keynes, whose prestige in the academic and political worlds had been built on a creative exploration of the boundaries of the period's economic "orthodoxy." To turn against one's church, apostasy, is always a worse crime than that of being a born atheist. Besides, Keynes was never a "pure" economist. He was intent on persuasion, publicly arguing out policies to improve the lives of actual people (and, also, of course, strengthening the international standing of Great Britain). Becoming a heretic may be intellectually amusing for some but Keynes not only knew the costs of heresy, but he also respected his forebears. In the early 1930s it was obvious he was *led* to seek new ways to understand the workings of modern economies by necessity rather than by pleasure.[1]

Keynes's stated reason to seek to establish new conceptual foundations for economic theory was the need to deal properly with the properties of money in modern economies and the implications of such a treatment to the understanding of how such economies actually operate. In *A Treatise on Money*, Keynes arrived at an impasse when he proposed that monetary factors affected the amount of investment an economy would spend on. Keynes had always accepted the Quantity Theory of Money[2] (hereafter QTM) as a theory of the long run impacts of changes in monetary policy on real and monetary variables. In the *Treatise* itself, his belief on the QTM was reaffirmed. But the QTM was based on a view of money as a mere means of payment, a vehicle for the purchase of the commodities individual agents wanted. Money was neutral because the choice of vehicles was, very reasonably, supposed to be independent of the choice of commodities to be bought with those vehicles. Once it changed hands in settlement of a market transaction, the role of money in the process was ended, leaving no permanent or durable mark on what happened afterwards. Only "real" factors mattered to determine the "real" choices of consumers and investors.

The *Treatise*, however, suggested that monetary factors actually did leave a durable mark on the "real" economic process. Affecting the amount of investment, monetary factors had an impact on the quantity of real capital accumulated in a given period, a central determinant of long-run configurations in practically all economic theories one can think of. But "classical" economic theory[3], of which the QTM was a fundamental pillar, was built on the idea that these effects did not exist. Keynes's first attempt to deal with such a dilemma was to circumvent it. In the *Tract on Monetary Reform*, Keynes wrote his famous dictum "in the long run we are all dead" to support his simultaneous attempts to give a substantive role to money in the short run while forgetting all about it in the long run. After the publication of the *Treatise* this view was no longer tenable. Examining where the dilemma was rooted, Keynes realized that it was in the very foundations of the dominant theories of the time. "Classical" economics, the theories that became dominant in Great Britain in the last decades of the nineteenth century, was based on a Robinson-Crusoe-concept of economy. An individual, solitary in an island lost somewhere in the middle of the ocean, has to decide how to survive under semi-wild conditions.[4] Crusoe had to choose between hunting and fishing, which gave different prizes since they yielded diverse levels of satisfaction, but demanded different amounts of effort. Moreover, he could postpone consumption while preparing better hunting and fishing instruments, illustrating how capital accumulation resulted from the interaction between Crusoe's intertemporal preferences and the production transformation possibilities opened by his technical knowledge and availability of instruments. A modern economy was assumed to be an immensely more complicated Crusoe-type economy, but not really of a different *nature*. In fact, in the same year the GT) was published, 1936, Roy Harrod's book *The Trade Cycle* came out, where this most typical phenomenon of *modern* industrial economies, the business cycle, was explained by reference to a modified Crusoe-type economy.

In the orthodox economist's reading of Defoe's text, Robinson Crusoe made choices between goods, by relating the satisfaction each class of goods offered to him against the effort needed to get them (his "budget constraint"). Following the same logic of behavior, he made choices as to how much capital he would produce and accumulate. Modern investors and consumers were supposed to behave according to the same logic. Crusoe economies, however, lacked money since there was no one else for Crusoe to deal with.[5] Therefore, there was no way money could be an essential factor in this type of economy, affecting consumption and investment choices. This was the conclusion Keynes seems to have finally arrived at, once the *Treatise* was published and was severely criticized by friends and foes alike.

Monetary economies

In 1933 Keynes gave few details of what the new conceptual framework would look like, but he informed readers what kind of result he expected from its use. He called the new framework a *monetary production economy*. Its main feature was to rely on the proposition that "real" variables were no longer sufficient to describe either short or long period equilibrium positions of the economy, in contrast to what he called the *cooperative economies* of classical economics, where monetary forces did not affect real equilibrium positions. Money, therefore, was no longer neutral in monetary production economies, not even in the long period, in the sense that

> ... the course of events cannot be predicted, either in the long period or in the short, without a knowledge of the behavior of money between the first state and the last. And it is this which we ought to mean when we speak of a monetary economy.
>
> (CW 13: 409)[6]

It is very important to stress, but also to clarify, this statement. For Keynes, the distinctive factor of a modern economy was that money played an essential role in it. To understand this role, it was necessary to identify and redefine the very foundations of the approach shared by dominant theories since they were all (or most) based on the idea that money is a late addition to the model, a qualification to be considered after everything essential to its workings had been identified and understood, as is done in a Crusoe-type economy. Keynes defended the idea that the results he wanted to stress could not be obtained by adding money to a fully structured "real" model, after its basic dynamics had already been determined.[7] To show why money was not neutral in the short as in the long period was proposed by Keynes to be the core of the theory of a monetary production economy.

Once the goal had been clearly established, the next step was to identify the fundamental features of existing modern economies that allowed money not to be neutral. Keynes's search for the elements that supported the non-neutrality of money was not systematic though, and it is not clear whether it could be.[8] It is also unclear if one could formulate the fundamental model in a simple and elegant way as is possible in the Crusoe tradition. But Keynes and those of his followers that pursued the same goal were able to outline which should be the essential traits of a monetary production economy, capable of guaranteeing the desired non-neutrality of money.

It should be made clear, perhaps, at the outset, that a theory of a monetary production economy is historically, or more precisely perhaps institutionally specific. Keynes followed Marshall's footsteps in understanding economics as an *evolutionary* discipline rejecting the radical ahistoricism proposed by Walras. Naturally, every economy faces the same fundamental problem of transforming natural resources into consumable output. Nevertheless, the way the economic activity is structured in order to solve that fundamental problem differs from one historical period to another, and from a type of social organization to another. One cannot elucidate how these economies work based only on "fundamental" notions. Keynes looked for a theory to explain the workings of *modern* economies, which he postulated to be structurally different from other types of economies, be those of the past, or those modern ones which were organized on different bases (such as the Soviet economy, contemporary to Keynes).

But Keynes would also develop an important *methodological* innovation. In the search for understanding the behavior of modern economies, Keynes would constantly move between two angles of approach. On the one hand, Keynes would ask himself what the individual decision-maker sees and how he or she processes the information received into the formation of expectations, how uncertainty is perceived and felt, and so on. Of course, he was not the only analyst taking this stand. Austrian economists also tried it, and Neo-Austrian economists proceed with this methodology. Keynes's novelty was to combine it with the Classical Political Economy, which was later followed by neoclassical equilibrium theorists, bird's eye view of the economy. In this angle of approach, the economist sees the economy as a *deus ex machina*, an outsider capable of seeing the whole picture at the same time, able, thus, to see how individuals interact, the extent to which such interactions constrain individual actions and confirm or negate expectations, etc. In other words, Keynes synthesizes the two methods of looking through the two alternative lenses, as an insider and as an outsider. Classical Political Economists tended to describe the great trends marking the development of capitalist economies. These trends were assumed to prevail no matter what individual agents thought or wanted. Radical individualists considered this nonsense, arguing that masses or social groups did not take decisions, individuals did. Keynes used both angles: the outsider view allows him to describe significant interactions between individual agents and the material and other constraints they face; the insider view allows him to see how individual decisions may shape these interactions and eventually change those constraints. For Keynes, there are no laws that impose themselves independently of the way individuals perceive constraints and set their goals. At the same time, individuals are not those absolute metaphysical entities, lost in time and space postulated by radical individualists. In the end, Keynes's method, fully utilized in the GT, is to begin with individuals, to ask himself what they see, what are they capable of understanding, how they feel their own limitations when making economic decisions, and then aggregate it all into theory of social interactions that shape collective behaviors.

In his attempts to name such an economy, Keynes tried some other denominations than monetary production economy. The terms *entrepreneurial economy*, *monetary economy* and *money wage economy* were also tried.[9] In this book we will use most frequently the term *entrepreneurial economy*, not only for shortness but also because it does focus attention right away on one of the fundamental features of the type of economy Keynes tried to define.

The most evident feature of an entrepreneurial economy is that its operation is led by firms. Firms tend to be a shadowy figure in modern economics. Conventional microeconomic theory usually reduces them to production functions, arguably a description of their "technical" side: a firm is the conduit through which inputs are transformed into outputs. Its "goal" is to maximize profits so that its owners can maximize their satisfaction by consuming a higher income than they would earn if each one tried to produce alone. Industrial organization studies, on the other hand, offer a more nuanced perspective of firms's motives and behaviors, but this is rarely integrated into "pure" theory.

Keynes never showed much interest in microeconomics one way or the other. Most of the time, Marshall's lessons in *The Principles of Economics* seemed to offer all he needed to know about firms. Nevertheless, when outlining his alternative to the Crusoe model of classical economics, the existence of firms and their central role in organizing production and capital accumulation seemed to mark the most fundamental difference between an economy describable through the production and consumption choices faced by a solitary individual and a modern economy, that is, an entrepreneurial economy. In his search for the key to understand why money is essential to the operation of a modern economy, Keynes, probably to his own surprise, got very close to Marx. Both thought that a capitalist firm is not a technical specification of how production is carried out, but a particular type of entity which pursues its own goals, which should not be confused with the goals of its owners or of its managers. Keynes approached the modern firm considering it an *individual*, defined by the particular object of its preferences: the control of wealth as such. As people demand specific consumption goods and are satisfied by their consumption, firms are proposed to demand wealth and to be satisfied with their accumulation. An important point of contrast between consumers and firms is that consumers increase their level of satisfaction when they can get hold of a varied basket of goods, while firms are not supposed to seek variety, because, again, it is wealth as such that they seek, in its most general form available.

The most general form of wealth in a market economy is money, which represents power to command a share of the incomes created in that economy at any time. Borrowing an expression from Marx, one can say that money is the *general* form of wealth, in contrast to the particular forms of wealth represented by stocks of specific goods which can only be expected to command social incomes if there is a solvable demand for those goods at a given particular moment.

The references to Marx are not gratuitous. They were, in fact, suggested by Keynes himself (CW 29: 81). When trying to clarify the nature and role of the firm in an entrepreneurial economy he appealed to Marx's well-known scheme of commodity circulation in a capitalist economy. Marx described it through a simple formula: $M \rightarrow C \rightarrow M'$, where M is the amount of money invested in the purchase of labor force and means of production at the beginning of the production cycle, C are the commodities produced during the cycle and M' is the surplus-value-added amount of money (M'>M) obtained at the end of the cycle, after the sale of output. Money is the beginning and the end of the process. Keynes borrows the idea stating that

> The firm is dealing throughout in terms of sums of money. It has no object in the world except to end up with more money than it started with. This is the essential characteristic of an entrepreneur economy.
>
> (CW 29: 89)

Firms are not supposed to accumulate money wealth because of money illusion, that is, the inability to distinguish "real" wealth from a pile of paper. They do so because the ability to sell a firm's output in the market means the social validation of that firm's activity. A firm may be very productive, employ state-of-the-art production methods and still fail if it is not able to sell its production for money. In Keynes's entrepreneurial economy approach, what matters to firms is less the ability to produce specific goods than the ability to generate and appropriate increasing amounts of wealth. The best index to measure this ability in real terms is the purchasing power of a firm's money revenues over labor units, the only input that is also of generalized use, employed in the production of any specific commodity. It is for this reason that money wages are so important a measure of "real" value in Keynes's theory. The focus on money wages is not simply an idiosyncratic choice of deflators made by Keynes, as some interpreters have thought, but an integral part of his theory.

The "theory" of the firm Keynes proposed would be, in fact, enough to establish the non-neutrality of money in such a class of economies. For firms, money is not a *means*, it is an *end*. Attaining this end depends not only on individual capacity, it depends also on liquidity conditions in the whole economy, and that is why it is not possible to describe short or long period positions of such an economy without knowledge of the monetary policy being implemented from the initial period to the last, as Keynes advanced in his 1933 manifesto launching the concept of monetary production economy.

Nevertheless, there were other features to this type of economy that might shape its dynamics in an essential way. To begin with, Keynes reckons that there is an "asymmetry of power" in such economies between households and firms. Firms are not only independent of households in setting their behavior, in the sense that they have their own preferences and goals, but they have also the stronger hand when dealing with them (relations with the third agent, governments, are murkier). This is made clear in the way Keynes describes the two markets where firms and households face directly each other, the labor market and the capital market. In the labor market, firms alone determine both the level of employment and the real wage, according to their revenue expectations. In the capital market, investing firms determine how much is going to be invested (and saved) in this type of economy, no matter what the intertemporal preferences of consumers are.

The full explanation for this power asymmetry is complex but can be reduced to two groups of arguments. First, firms make their production and investment decisions based on their short and long term net revenue expectations. Households are supposed to be much more reactive, adapting to current stimuli rather than anticipating the future. Second, and even more important, firms are not constrained by current income in the same degree as households. Firms have a strong and systematic access to credit, which makes their spending largely discretionary. Thus, both in terms of motives and of possibilities, firms' decisions are relatively autonomous with respect to current developments while households are usually assumed to "adapt" to, rather than to lead, these developments. When government is introduced, later in the analysis, it will share similar characteristics with firms, only in a more concentrated way, and this will be the foundation of Keynes's characteristic theory of economic policy.

Firms, households and government are supposed to operate in a context of uncertainty. As has been stressed by generations of Keynesian economists, uncertainty cannot be reduced to calculable risk. Keynes insisted on the important distinction between situations similar to games of chance, where the universe of future events is known and a definite numerical probability can be attributed to each of them, and fundamental uncertainty, where unpredicted and *unpredictable* events can happen. Of course, the future is not more uncertain in entrepreneurial economies than in cooperative (or other types of) economies. The point is that in entrepreneurial economies the costs of a wrong decision are borne by private individuals (be they actual persons or entities). Under these conditions, it is *rational* for these individuals to adopt defensive forms of behavior that could seem irrational under calculable risks conditions. All of Keynes's major theoretical innovations in the GT consist of either the identification of types of defensive behavior (liquidity preference, precautionary savings, conventional behavior, and so on) or of pointing out the consequences of the adoption of defensive behaviors (deficient effective demand, involuntary unemployment, etc.).

Many authors have chosen to emphasize how uncertainty can make monetary economies unstable, prone to sudden collapses, mainly through the fall of investments. Keynes himself seemed to be more impressed by the actual *stability* shown by these economies than by the ever-present possibilities of a sudden collapse. In part, Keynes seemed to think that the observed stability of modern economies was due to a seemingly accidental combination of values of the parameters of the main overall behavioral functions of the economy.[10] Authors like Paul Davidson stressed the importance of the emergence of institutions designed to reduce uncertainty, either by coordinating individual decisions and plans or to socialize the costs of making mistaken decisions. In particular, Davidson has insisted on the strategic role played by the widespread system of money forward contracts underlying the organization of production and, to some extent, sales in such economies.

In any case, as Keynes himself warned, in the GT, especially in its Chapter 12, ensuring permanent systemic stability may be an impossible task. In fact, many institutions created to reduce some classes of uncertainty ended up exposing economies to other sources of uncertainty, as Keynes exemplified in his vivid discussion of the repercussions of the creation of Stock Exchanges. The possibility that stability itself may nurture instability was the starting point of Hyman Minsky's theory of financial fragility.

Be it as it may, Keynes was less impressed by the cyclical fluctuations of modern capitalism than by possibility of an entrepreneurial economy to remain in an unsatisfactory state, with high involuntary unemployment, for example, for a prolonged period. Such economies seemed to be unable to move out of such a fix by their own internal forces, the situation most of the developed world seemed to be experiencing in the 1930s. Significant involuntary unemployment showed itself to be compatible with "equilibrium," in the sense that neither workers, nor employers, not any other social group in society would see any way to change the situation.

For decades, after the end of World War II, Keynes's concerns seemed to be somewhat obsolete. Cyclical, not persistent, unemployment seemed to be the problem of advanced entrepreneurial economies, at least until the late 1980s, when unemployment rose to high levels in Western Europe and remained high for years.[11] High employment and inflation seemed to be much more important problems of that age than those which worried Keynes. Writing from a different time perspective, Hyman Minsky was inspired by these changes to advance the notion of *coherence* to deal with change within stable environments (Minsky, 1980). Coherence means the absence of major disequilibria, a situation where individual plans are reasonably coordinated so that short-term expectations tend to be generally confirmed. Confirmation, however, did not lead to *stasis*. In fact, one of the novelties of Minsky's approach is precisely that *stability is destabilizing*, perhaps the most famous of his aphorisms. Precautions cost money. Typical precautions (which Minsky called *safety margins*) include keeping liquid assets, such as money, in the portfolio, pre-contracting contingent credit lines, neglecting more profitable opportunities of investment which may also be riskier, etc. When experiencing longer periods of stability, people tend to forget the reasons that originally explained why those precautions were adopted. All that is left in evidence is the cost of hedging or the lost profit opportunities. If people convince themselves that precautions were at least partially unnecessary, they will make riskier bets, and the economy will become more and more *incoherent*. Increasing incoherence means that the economy becomes less resilient in the face of adverse shocks, since it cannot absorb disappointments without causing large losses to decision-makers. In his financial fragility theory, Minsky shows that prosperity breeds increasing speculation and rising risk exposure until one gets to a situation where even a small shock may drive the economy into a crisis.

Money and liquidity preference

Whether entrepreneurial economies are inherently stable or unstable and whether stability can coexist with problems like high involuntary unemployment and stagnation are central questions to the paradigm known as Post Keynesian economics, particularly the strand inspired by Keynes's own writings. Spawning these themes is the concept of fundamental uncertainty referred to above. The central proposition is that uncertainty leads individuals (again, actual persons or entities, such as firms) to take precautions when they decide on a course of action. Several kinds of institutions have been created and policies have been designed to lighten the burden of uncertainty on individuals but they cannot eliminate it altogether. Individuals still have to seek efficient ways to hedge their choices. Sometimes, what looks efficient to an individual may have disastrous social consequences if adopted by large numbers of individuals. Exploring the wider consequences of the adoption of individually-efficient hedging strategies was, and still is, a central theme of the GT and of Keynesian economics in general.

How does one make decisions when one cannot be sure about the consequences of that decision had been a theme of a lifelong interest for Keynes. It was the subject of the more ambitious of his early works, the *Treatise on Probability*. It was only when writing the GT, however, that he seemed to finally identify the deep implications the serious consideration of uncertainty would have for monetary theory and macroeconomics.

In parallel to his works on more abstract theoretical issues, Keynes had also dedicated a permanent attention to money, and related issues, such as monetary standards, regimes and policies, exchange and interest rates, liquidity, etc. Keynes's approach was shaped by his Marshallian training: rather than exploring properties of monetary equilibrium states, his work always focused on adjustment mechanisms, the movements *between* equilibrium states. Up until the preparation of the GT, Keynes inhabited the world of the Quantity Theory of Money, but the theory itself seemed to be the object of reverence rather than a guide to his thinking about monetary problems. The QTM postulated that, in the long run, money prices were determined by the supply of money. In that state, real variables, that is, to the exclusion of monetary forces, determined "real" outcomes, and nominal variables determined only nominal outcomes. During transitional periods, between two equilibrium positions, monetary variables could have a real impact. This impact, however, was due either to some price rigidities (for instance, those embodied in contracts) or to the difficulty of individuals to see through the "money veil" which led them to sometimes take monetary changes for real changes. Both difficulties were considered short-term obstacles, though, to be surmounted by the passage of time. When full equilibrium was finally reached, in the long run, all of these difficulties would have been properly dealt with and money would be neutral again. Money only mattered during the transitional periods.

But it was in the transition periods that resided Keynes's challenges in the period before the publication of the GT, the situations where "real" and "monetary" variables were actually mixed. As we saw above, it was only after the *Treatise on Money* was published that Keynes finally realized that this strategy of dealing with "real" influences of monetary forces while at the same time maintaining the QTM as a description of long run equilibrium states was untenable.

In the *Treatise*, Keynes took his theoretical innovations to what he seemed to think were the boundaries of the QTM.[12] He proposed that money circulation, traditionally treated by the QTM as a unified circuit, should be broken in two: industrial circulation and financial circulation. The first dealt with the circulation of goods and services, which were the standard ground of the QTM. The second dealt with the circulation of financial assets. Formally, the two circulations differed because they entailed different money velocities, relying as they were on different classes of transactions. Industrial circulation depended on characteristics of the general economy such as the timing of contractual payments (especially wages). Financial circulation depended on more complex mechanisms related to expectations as to the future behavior of asset prices. In the financial circulation, "bears," those expecting a fall in the prices of securities in the relevant future, would keep idle balances while "bulls," a group defined by the opposite expectations, would buy financial assets. As Keynes insisted, there was no necessary connection between the two velocities. Overall velocity, the one present in the Equation of Exchange (v in $Mv = Py$) would be just a weighted average of the two actual velocities, without any theoretical or empirical explanatory value.

Keynes advanced in the *Treatise*, therefore, a *systemic* perspective to approach the roles money plays in modern economies and derived many important lessons from it. A particularly important lesson was that deflationary pressures may emerge in such economies as a result of the shift of money from industrial circulation to financial circulation even if total money supply remained the same. In fact, although financial and industrial circulations were largely autonomous in their workings, they were still related because financial assets prices, determined in the former, affected "real" investment spending and therefore incomes and output in industrial circulation. In fact, this was one of the most important "transmission mechanisms" of monetary policy to real variables, but changes of a similar nature could happen spontaneously. If bearish sentiment, for instance, for any reason, became dominant in financial circulation, interest rates would be pushed upwards attracting money from industrial circulation and creating deflationary pressures on the "real" economy.

The two-circuits of money circulation represented an improvement over the traditional methods of the QTM, but they still relied on the notion that money is just a means of payment. In other words, money is still held by individuals only in anticipation of definite expenditure plans. The introduction of the notion of financial circulation, however, opened a new avenue, where individuals hold money for (perhaps indefinitely) longer periods of time, since neither bears or bulls can know *when* prices will move in the direction they expect, and thus they don't know *when* they will spend their money balances. But Keynes would still take some time before arriving at his final consideration of money as an asset itself, and therefore not as a vehicle but as an end. Writing in 1937 in response to critics, Keynes identified this final view as the first of the two main innovations of the GT.

The main obstacle to be overcome at this point, to finally abandon the QTM, was to establish the properties of money that made it an asset, that is, a form of wealth, an object of demand itself instead of serving merely of vehicle for the demand of something else. Of course, money is durable, it can survive more than one period, and can, therefore, be accumulated like any other real or financial asset. But, Keynes rhetorically asked himself in 1937, why would anybody hold money as an asset?[13]

Keynes proposed that money becomes an asset, therefore, because under fundamental uncertainty *money offers the safest way to accumulate wealth*. As purchasing power in "pure" form, independent of any specific market demands (as it happens with other types of assets), money exhibits the highest *liquidity attribute* among all forms of wealth. Liquidity means the power to change form, to be convertible into something else. Under uncertainty, being liquid means that the asset offers insurance against what is uninsurable otherwise, because it allows the liquid asset holder to convert it into cash, buy something else and start over.

Keynes first developed this argument in the famous Chapter 17 of the GT, where he proposed that assets that are less liquid than money have to pay a premium to compensate for their relative illiquidity in the form of an interest rate so they can attract money holders and make them to part with money. Every asset price, therefore, is determined by two components: expected money yields (incomes and capital gains) and liquidity *premia*. The availability of money or the easiness of access to money determines the market value of liquidity and thus affects directly the prices of all other assets. *Money is not neutral in the long period because it affects "real" capital accumulation through the pricing of real capital assets.*[14]

To maintain its liquidity higher than any other asset, the availability of money in entrepreneurial economies has to be constrained. In a sense, for an asset to be liquid simply means to remain in a permanent state of excess demand. Money, to be as liquid as it has to be in entrepreneurial economies, has to be *rare*, otherwise individuals can be *saturated* of money as it happens with any other class of assets or goods. The implications of such an assumption for the operation of the monetary system, and to monetary policy in particular, are explored in Chapter 4 of this book.

In sum, liquidity preference, the theory according to which asset prices are determined by expectations of money yields and by their liquidity *premia*, is a theory of capital accumulation rather than merely a theory of money demand, or an unnecessarily original way of presenting the old QTM, as some critics frequently argue. In the approach followed in this book, it is in fact the core of the Keynesian reconstruction of economic theory initiated with the publication of the GT and other of Keynes's works, and continued by many others, particularly, but certainly not exclusively, Post Keynesians.[15]

The possibilities opened by the concept of liquidity preference presented by Keynes are multifold. The first generation of Keynesian economists, including his younger contemporaries like Richard Kahn and Joan Robinson, explored or developed many of the central arguments mentioned here. Authors such as Paul Davidson explored the foundations of the concept of liquidity (including, with emphasis, the creation of a system of forward money contracts) and the properties of money necessary to preserve its liquid nature. Hyman Minsky extended

Keynes's analysis of asset choice and pricing to full balance sheet choices, introducing the notion that perhaps even more important than discussing the liquidity of specific classes of assets may be the examination of the liquidity of *balance sheets as a whole*. These and other aspects of Keynes's theories were further developed (and applied to the study of current events) by Jan Kregel, Victoria Chick, Sheila Dow and Paul Wells, just to mention a few of the pioneers.[16]

The most important implication of this theory was developed, however, by Keynes himself: the theory of effective demand. In a nutshell, when the demand for liquid assets increases (because of a rise in perceived uncertainties, for instance, or because of a collapse of the marginal efficiency of capital),[17] at the expense of the demand for reproducible assets, such as capital goods, the loss of employment in the production of investment goods cannot be made up for by an increase in the employment in the production of liquid assets, notably money. The impact of the original loss of income and employment on total income is magnified by the consumption multiplier, so consumption falls in solidarity with investment (instead of rising to compensate the fall of investment, as assumed in classical economics). Involuntary unemployment then ensues and remain in existence as long as the demand for goods remain prostrated. The vicious circle can then only be broken by an external agent, not constrained by uncertainties of the future and access to money, which is the foundation of Keynes's theory of economic policy, discussed in Chapter 8.

The plan of the book

All the issues listed in this chapter will be further examined in this book. The method chosen is to start with a historical approach, where we identify the foundations of Keynes's liquidity preference theory based on his own original ideas. We then evaluate criticisms raised against the original propositions or developments proposed to extend them to give a picture of how the theory should be understood in the present. At the end of the book, we propose our own extensions of the liquidity preference approach, first to deal with the determination of economic policies that are expected to be efficient in monetary economies as conceived by Keynes and those who followed his steps, and, in the last chapter, to illustrate how well the theory performs when applied to situations like the financial crisis of 2007–2008 and its aftermath.

The next chapter deals with the most fundamental issue treated in this area, how uncertainty should be understood and how can one formulate a theory of demand for liquid assets, more particularly for money assets, under such circumstances. It is shown that Keynes himself seemed to be uncertain as how to do it and his arguments ended up being presented in a somewhat confuse or even inconsistent way in the GT. We critically examine how two prominent Keynesian economists, Richard Kahn and James Tobin, tried to improve on Keynes's own original formulation.

Chapter 3 stresses the centrality of the notion of liquidity premium in Keynes's theory, by examining how other risks are dealt with in the GT, and why liquidity risk is selected for special treatment. Besides examining the arguments present in the GT, we speculate about the reasons for the prominence of liquidity risks in the analysis of asset pricing offered by Keynes.

While one can say that Chapters 2 and 3 deal with the demand for assets, and particularly for liquid assets, Chapters 4 and 5 turn to the ways money is created and introduced in the economy. Chapter 4 focuses on a debate that emerged some years after Keynes's death, initiated by Nicholas Kaldor, which increased in importance through the years, centered on the question of whether the expression "quantity of money" makes any sense, theoretically and as a target for monetary policy. Kaldor's and Keynes's views are contrasted and related to each one's wider theoretical horizons.

Chapter 5 extends the discussion initiated in Chapter 4, focusing on the question of how banks' decisions affect money supply. Based on ideas developed by Keynes mostly in the *Treatise on Money*, it is shown that in this theoretical approach banks hold a key not only to the quantity of money that is created but also the way it is allocated in the economy. It is shown that banks' behavior, in this particular, is a crucial element of an understanding of the effects of financial crises.

Chapter 6 changes the focus to the problem of financing private expenditures, more particularly of private investments. It is probably universally recognized that Keynes's arguments about the relationship between saving and investment fell into oblivion. Orthodox macroeconomics neglect the problem entirely, but even non-orthodox economics exhibit some profound disagreement on how that relationship should be understood. The chapter offers an explanation of the relationship, based on the liquidity preference approach, by confronting Keynes to Wicksell, perhaps the most important author in the "classical" tradition on this matter.

Chapter 7, on the other hand, concentrates on the examination of a notion that rises in interest whenever a major financial crisis occurs, the question of systemic risk and systemic crisis. In that chapter we critically review some of the dominant views as to the meaning of systemic risk and systemic crisis. We then explore the foundations of a Keynesian alternative understanding of these phenomena and outline its implications for the design of prudential regulation.

In Chapter 8, as already mentioned, we change again our focus, to concentrate less on monetary and financial problems *per se* to attack, from a Keynesian theoretical perspective, the problem of which policies are more adequate to improve the performance of monetary economies.

Finally, Chapter 9 concludes the book by illustrating how liquidity preference theory performs in a concrete, real situation, that of the financial crisis of 2007–2008, its contagion to the European Union and its aftermath.

Chapters 1, 3 and 9 were written for this volume, while the remaining chapters were adapted and updated from papers already published (see the list in the acknowledgements). In the adaptation for use in this volume, I tried to reduce repetitions to the extent possible. Some concepts, though, need to be reintroduced in some chapters in order to frame the argument that follows. Constantly cross-referencing and sending the reader back to a unique place in the text where those concepts were first introduced would probably be more laborious and bothersome.

Notes

1 In fact, as it can be easily seen by comparing the early drafts of the GT, published in volumes 13 and 29 of Keynes's Collected Writings, with the finally printed book, the most aggressive or intellectually innovative arguments he planned to present had their edges significantly softened as time went by.
2 See Kahn (1984: 53), quoted in Chapter 4.
3 See Chapter 2, below for Keynes's special meaning of the label "classical."
4 Robinson Crusoe, in fact, was not entirely solitary. He could draw on what England of his time could offer as capital since the ship where he was traveling was stranded in the rocks near enough the island to allow him to get essential supplies from its cargo.
5 One should remember that Man Friday was a slave.
6 "On my view, there is no unique long-period position of equilibrium equally valid regardless of the character of the policy of the monetary authority" (CW 29: 55).
7 "The idea that it is comparatively easy to adapt the hypothetical conclusions of a real wage [classical] economics to the real world of monetary economics is a mistake" (CW 13: 410).
8 Davidson (1984) tried to build an axiomatic structure to support Keynes's concept of monetary economy, but the three axioms he proposed were subject to wide criticism. In Cardim de Carvalho (1992), Chapter 3, I tried to outline a more flexible structure of fundamental postulates, but I am no longer satisfied with it.
9 While he called *cooperative economies* or *real wage economies* the model underlying classical economics in the drafts of the GT.
10 Keynes did mention more than once in the GT the possibility of "collapses" in the marginal efficiency of capital leading to declines in income and employment. But it was the overall stability of the system and the rarity of occasions when catastrophic declines took place that impressed him the most. See Chapter 18 of the GT. One should keep in mind that the stability of modern capitalism that impressed Keynes was not an unambiguous advantage: Keynes noted that although catastrophes were rate, modern economies could remain stable for long periods in very unsatisfactory positions, with, for instance, very high rates of unemployment.
11 Then, as in the 1930s, many economists argued that it was structural unemployment.
12 It is not entirely clear whether Keynes really believed the scheme advanced in the *Treatise* to be compatible with the QTM or he was just making a *petitio principi* that it was so to avoid the discussion.
13 The question, and Keynes's answer, are discussed in detail in the next chapter.
14 Curiously, Keynes initially downplayed the demand for money as such, not as a means of payment in the chapters of the GT dealing with the motives to demand liquid assets or to demand money. The implications of such a decision is the subject of Chapter 2 of this book.
15 See Kregel (1988) for a development of this point in the context of Hicks's reconstruction of Keynes's theory in the IS/LM model.
16 One should be careful here to point out that these authors do not necessarily see themselves as "members of a school." What is being stated is that their works can fit without problems in a theoretical perspective such as the one described in this chapter.
17 Which is the expected rate of return on "real" investment.

Part I
Money and uncertainty

2   Uncertainty and liquidity preference

1 Introduction

The publication of the GT generated several public debates. Keynes, however, got personally involved in only a few of them. For one of these, Keynes wrote the article "The General Theory of Employment," published in 1937, to refute criticisms coming from a number of economists, chiefly among whom were Wassily Leontief and Jacob Viner. In that paper, Keynes argued that there were two main theoretical novelties in the GT, one of which was the examination between money demand and uncertainty.[1]

As is well known, Keynes in the 1937 paper advanced a specific concept of uncertainty, to be contrasted to the most commonly accepted treatment of risk within a framework of calculable probabilities. Keynes was concerned with situations where it is not possible even to conceive the universe of possible outcomes of a given process, a requisite he had already established in the *Treatise on Probability* (CW 8), for the attribution of *a priori* numerical probabilities. In his view, when facing this kind of uncertainty, agents could not protect themselves, even in theory, through the usual appeal to insurance. Therefore, to seek protection against uncertainty, agents had to find instruments that could be activated in situations that could not, however, be specified in an insurance policy. Keynes postulated that, in an entrepreneurial or monetary economy, this protection would be given by the possession of money.

If this was true, important consequences would ensue for the dynamics of entrepreneurial economies, including its proneness to generate involuntary unemployment. Basically, involuntary unemployment would emerge when the public demanded money, which Keynes postulated in the GT to be non-reproducible, instead of capital goods, the production of which demanded the employment of labor. This was stated by Keynes to be the first of the two major theoretical innovations of the GT that had eluded keen critics like Leontief or Viner.

Keynes faulted his critics for having misunderstood his point[2], but one cannot but wonder, however, how clearly or forcefully this argument had been really presented in the GT. In fact, not only classically-trained economists like Leontief or Viner had problems in identifying the connection proposed by Keynes between money demand and uncertainty. Authors who went on to become leading interpreters of the Keynesian tradition, like Richard Kahn, Keynes's own closest collaborator, and James Tobin, in the American Keynesian school, also felt the need to modify Keynes's original presentation in the GT. In this chapter, we revisit Keynes's discussion of money demand in the GT and see how effectively the theory proposed there fulfilled the intentions he clarified in the 1937 article. We also want to use Kahn's 1954 and Tobin's 1958 seminal contributions to help clarify the difficulties faced even by sympathetic readers of the GT when interpreting that theory.

We begin by discussing Keynes's stated intentions in his "General Theory of Employment" article, to contrast them with the actual treatment given in the GT. This occupies Section 2 of this chapter. In Section 3, we examine Kahn's criticisms and proposed modifications, doing the same with respect to Tobin's 1958 article in Section 4. Section 5 closes the chapter with a summary of the main arguments and their implications, including for the modern debate on the workings of monetary policy.

2 Keynes on uncertainty and money

As already mentioned, Keynes, in his "The General Theory of Employment," of 1937, criticized some of the initial reviewers of the GT for their inability to understand his meaning of uncertainty and its implications for the behavior of economic agents, especially with respect to wealth accumulation. As is frequently the case, however, it is possible to counter-argue that those relationships were clearer to Keynes himself than to those who knew Keynes's ideas only through reading the GT. Certainly, Keynes's views on uncertainty are clearer to those who are also acquainted with his *Treatise on Probability*. It is debatable, though, whether the GT alone fully conveys the meaning that Keynes attributed to the concept of uncertainty. Be that as it may, in his 1937 paper, Keynes tried to spell out unequivocally, if yet not very precisely, what he understood by uncertainty and what its implications were for the connection between wealth accumulation and money demand.

Keynes's 1937 argument on uncertainty and money demand[3]

Despite the centrality of the concept of uncertainty to the argument presented in his 1937 paper and its differences with the notion of calculable risk, Keynes curiously refrained from defining it precisely. Mostly, he appealed to intuitive notions suggested by statements like "actually, however, we have, as a rule, only the vaguest idea of any but the most direct consequences of our acts" (CW 14: 113).

In one of his best-known passages, Keynes may in fact be said to define uncertainty by exclusion and by examples:

> By uncertain knowledge, let me explain, I do not mean merely to distinguish what is known for certain from what is only probable. The game of roulette

is not subject, in this sense, to uncertainty; nor is the prospect of a Victory bond being drawn. Or, again, the expectation of life is only slightly uncertain. Even the weather is only moderately uncertain. The sense in which I am using the term is that in which the prospect of a European war is uncertain, or the price of copper and the rate of interest twenty years hence, or the obsolescence of a new invention, or the position of private wealth owners in the social system in 1970. About these matters there is no *scientific basis* on which to form any calculable probability whatever. We simply don't know.

> (CW 14: 113–114, my emphasis)

The "scientific basis" to which Keynes refers was the information necessary to calculate probabilities, which should allow the reduction of "uncertainty to the same calculable status as that of certainty itself" (CW 14: 112–113).

Probabilities cannot be calculated when it is not possible to identify the full set of events that *can* result from a given cause, so one cannot say, with certainty, that one element of that particular set of outcomes *will* definitely result from that cause. Keynes makes it clear that it is not just a question of possibly overwhelming complexity of calculations, as is the case of, for instance, weather forecasting. It is rather a question that, with social processes, *uncaused causes*, to use Shackle's expression, may operate as true innovations, that is, as unpredictable ruptures with past experience making a given development process unique. Uncertainty causes any element of knowledge liable to possibly become suddenly obsolete when an unpredicted and unpredictable new cause operated to change the course of a given process.[4] Knowing that the future is uncertain, human beings' expectations tend to be unstable and subject to drastic and sudden change, making any commitment to specific future scenarios inherently risky.

Keynes argued that uncertainty was a stronger influence in processes that could extend into the longer term:

> Thus the fact that our knowledge of the future is fluctuating, vague and uncertain, renders wealth a peculiarly unsuitable subject for the methods of classical economic theory.
>
> (CW 14: 113)

Classical methods were those Keynes associated either with certainty or with calculable risks.[5]

The point Keynes was making was not immediately clear at the time even to his closest collaborators. As Kahn observed, in commenting the paper before publication: "there is nothing to explain why the hypothesis of a calculable future would, if legitimate, result in full employment" (CW 14: 108). Nowadays, however, we don't need to dwell any further on the matter.[6]

It is important to notice that Keynes was not just proposing that at least some economic processes could be conceived as indeterminate, but stressing the fact agents *knew* them to be uncertain. In fact, it was the *behavior* of economic agents that interested Keynes to the extent that those behaviors were shaped by the *feeling* of uncertainty. In fact, the demand for money, at least in part, would be explained by the *perception of true uncertainty* rather than the *fact* of uncertainty, something the "classical school" simply could not really understand:[7]

> partly on reasonable and partly on instinctive grounds, our desire to hold money as a store of wealth is a barometer of *the degree of our distrust* or our own calculations and conventions concerning the future.
>
> (CW 14: 116, my emphasis)

Money in an entrepreneurial economy, being the means through which any contractual obligation is settled, is purchasing power in general form.[8] If the future is uncertain in the sense of the term that Keynes proposed, one needs protection against unspecified and unspecifiable adverse future events.[9] Only the possession of money can offer a blanket protection against future disappointments of economic expectations. As a consequence:

> [t]he possession of actual money lulls our disquietude; and the premium which we require to make us part with money is the measure of the *degree of our disquietude*.
>
> (CW 14: 116, my emphasis)

It is important to notice that, for Keynes, only when one deals with true uncertainty can one speak of *disquietude* or *confidence*, since it is only in this case that the decision-maker has to be conscious of the limitations under which any prediction of future events is made.[10] The higher perceived uncertainty is, the lower will be the confidence on one's expectation and the higher will be one's degree of disquietude with respect to the future.[11]

In the 1937 paper, thus, the theory Keynes proposed to explain the interest rate was based on the interaction between the demand for hoards, derived from the search for protection against uncertainty, and the supply of hoards by the banking system. For a given quantity of money, "[t]he rate of interest is the factor which adjusts at the margin the demand for hoards to the supply of hoards" (CW 14: 117). Thus, again for a given quantity of money, "fluctuations in the *degree of confidence*" affect "not the amount that is actually hoarded, but the amount of the premium which has to be offered to induce people not to hoard" (CW 14: 116, my emphasis).

As Keynes had already done in the GT, he assumed in the 1937 paper that the quantity of money was fixed by the monetary authority.[12] The demand for hoards would then determine, given the supply, the interest rate that the marginal efficiency of capital had to top if new investment was to be realized and employment in the capital goods sector to be generated to reach full employment when desired savings were positive. The concern with the behavior of investment took Keynes to the second part of his paper, where he discussed the consumption multiplier and the determination of aggregate income.

One should notice that in "The General Theory of Employment" Keynes did not use the language he himself proposed in the GT to classify the modalities of (or motives for) money demand. In particular, he did not distinguish between precautionary and speculative demands for money. He contrasted money required by "the active circulation for the transaction of current business" to "inactive balances, i.e. for hoards" (CW 14: 117). The demand for hoards was explained at least three times in the paper as a reaction to the *lack of confidence* in expectations about the future, as shown in the three quotations reproduced above on this point.

In sum, Keynes criticized his classical commentators in this paper for not having noticed that his argument in the GT was that:

1   uncertainty caused a demand for money to emerge to satisfy the public's lack of confidence in their expectations about the future, beyond the traditionally recognized demand for means of payment or active balances;
2   that the interest rate was a measure of this degree of confidence, since it measured the reward wealth-holders demanded for parting with liquidity and the reward should increase with uncertainty; and
3   that when uncertainty rose, therefore, all else remaining the same, interest rates would go up and investment in capital goods would fall.

This line of argument was complemented in part two of the 1937 paper by the examination of the consumption multiplier showing that the impact of the fall of investment on aggregate demand would be higher than the value of the fall of investment itself. This sequence of arguments constitute the *general theory of employment* Keynes was proposing in the GT but in his judgment it had escaped classical critics. How fair was Keynes's criticism of his critics?

Keynes on liquidity preference in the GT

In the GT, the demand for money is presented in Chapters 13 to 15, dealing with the determination of the interest rate. Keynes had already introduced in previous chapters the notions of the *consumption multiplier*, which made aggregate demand depend on the volume of investment, and of *marginal efficiency of capital*, whereby investment was shown to depend on the interest rate (for a given state of long-term expectations). One of the central points of the GT was, in fact, to show that the interest rate is not the price that brings investment and savings into equality, but that "[i]t is the 'price' which equilibrates the desire to hold wealth in the form of cash with the available quantity of cash" (CW 7: 167). Thus, the interest rate is proposed to be "the reward for parting with liquidity for a specified period" (CW 7: 167) instead of being the reward for waiting or for abstention from present consumption, as proposed in the classical tradition.[13]

A liquidity-preference schedule could then be identified as "a potentiality or functional tendency, which fixes the quantity of money which the public will hold when the rate of interest is given; so that if r is the rate of interest, M the quantity of money and L the function of liquidity-preference, we have $M = L(r)$" (CW 7: 168).

Liquidity preference, therefore, is defined in terms of the exposure to yet undefined risks that parting with liquidity implies for a wealth-holder.[14] Liquidity preference is initially introduced as a result of a "precautionary motive" and of a "speculative motive." Three pages later in the same chapter, Keynes modified his definition of liquidity, to make the concept of liquidity preference also to include the "transactions motive" (CW 7: 170).[15]

Both the precautionary and the speculative motives are proposed to result from "the existence of *uncertainty* as to the future of the rate of interest" (CW 7: 168, emphasis in the original). The precautionary motive refers, in Chapter 13, to "the risk of disappointment" of "[t]he actuarial profit or mathematical expectation of gain calculated in accordance with the existing probabilities – if it can be so calculated ..." (CW 7: 169). The speculative motive to hold money, on the other hand, emerges when some wealth holders believe that interest rates will rise in the future (CW 7: 170), as it was the case of *bears*, as Keynes, following market usage, called them in *A Treatise on Money* (CW 5).

The speculative motive was supposed, thus, to lead to clearly identifiable and predictable actions on the part of wealth holders: bears held money in anticipation of a fall in the price of securities and bulls did the opposite because the latter expected those prices to rise. The precautionary motive, in contrast, was defined in somewhat fuzzy fashion: while it was first presented as arising from uncertainty about the disappointment of profit expectations in one page of the GT (CW 7: 169), it was defined as a reaction to the uncertainty about the marketability of a given debt in the next (CW 7: 170).

Uncertainty, in fact, affected both the precautionary and the speculative motives, but in different ways, a point that would be stressed by Kahn, as we will see later in this chapter.[16] One could perhaps say that it is the uncertainty *felt by each person* that leads her to demand money for precautionary reasons. Systemic uncertainty, on the other hand, is the foundation for the speculative motive: neither bulls nor bears are, *a priori*, correct in their expectations. The position the system will take (and therefore whose expectations will turn out right) will depend on the relative market strength of each group.

In addition, both the speculative and the precautionary motives are affected by the existence and degree of organization of markets for existing debts:

> ... in the absence of an organized market, liquidity-preference due to the precautionary motive would be greatly increased; whereas the existence of an organized market gives an opportunity for wide fluctuations in liquidity preference due to the speculative-motive.
>
> (CW 7: 171)

The existence of secondary markets for existing debts should affect the precautionary demand for money to the extent that, in the presence of such markets, holding interest-earning debts would be less risky to some degree, reducing the attractiveness of yieldless money. On the other hand, the possibility of changes in the prices of debts occurring frequently in such markets open up opportunities to speculate with possible future values of such contracts, feeding the speculative demand for money.

The motives to demand money will reemerge in Chapter 15 of the GT. In the latter, Keynes formally defined three motives to demand money:

1   the transactions motive, comprising the income motive (pertaining basically for households) and the business motive (demand for money by firms willing to engage in transactions with goods and services);
2   the precautionary motive; and
3   the speculative motive.

The transactions demand is defined in the traditional way. It is the quantity of money demanded in anticipation of payments for goods and services and, for a given structure of contractual payments in the economy, depends upon current income on the assumption of a stable velocity of circulation.

The precautionary motive is defined as providing "for contingencies requiring sudden expenditure and for unforeseen opportunities of advantageous purchases, and also to hold an asset of which the value is fixed in terms of money to meet a subsequent liability fixed in terms of money ..." (CW 7: 196). It is striking that neither confidence, disquietude or even uncertainty itself are mentioned as central factors operating through the precautionary motive.

Before introducing the speculative motive, however, Keynes takes an unexpected turn. Arguing that both the transactions and the precautionary motives "will partly depend on the cheapness and the reliability of methods of obtaining cash, when it is required" and will also be influenced by "the relative cost of holding cash," Keynes states that "[i]n normal circumstances the amount of money required to satisfy the transactions motive *and the precautionary motive* is mainly a resultant of the general activity of the economic system and of the level of money income" (CW 7: 196, my emphasis).

In other words, the precautionary motive became a variation of the transactions motive that can be omitted from the argument without much loss of substance. Uncertainty-shaped precautions taken by agents simply disappeared from the model as an independent form of behavior! The demand for money explained by uncertainty *as such*, that is, by the degree of disquietude of the public or by the lack of confidence on one's own expectations, which Keynes only a year later will propose to be essential, one of the two revolutionary innovations of the GT, was tossed away, subsumed in that most traditional of concepts, the transactions motive to hold money, so cherished by the quantity theory of money.

In fact, nothing is said about how those elements related to the notion of uncertainty could be subsumed in the concept of income, which, being the determinant of the transactions motive to demand money, also became the explicit determinant of the precautionary demand for money in the GT. No wonder classical critics of the GT did not see why the relationship between money and uncertainty was so important to Keynes's argument! They could not see it because in the GT Keynes buried it in the old quantity theory of money.[17]

The speculative demand for money is defined in Chapter 15 in a similar way to what is offered in Chapter 13. Each wealth holder is presented with the possibility of buying debt or holding money. If a given agent judges the current rate of interest to be lower than what is expected to be the "normal" rate of interest, he will hold money to avoid suffering capital losses in the future, when the interest rate does rise back to its normal level and the price of debt falls. If he judges the current rate to be above the normal rate, he will hold securities instead of money.

In this context, the liquidity function will be defined by two components L_1 and L_2 and

$$M = M_1 + M_2 = L_1(Y) + L_2(r)$$

Again, no word is said about the influence of uncertainty, confidence or any other variable related to them.[18]

The question cannot be avoided: why did Keynes, who later wrote that confidence in expectations in a context of uncertainty was the main factor to explain why people hoard money, and therefore to explain the level of the interest rate, choose to concentrate in the GT instead on a modality of money demand, the speculative demand for money, which is explained by agents holding *definite* expectations as to future interest rates?[19] Why did he neglect the very factor he would later state to be the key element to mark the difference between his and the classical theory?

The hypothesis we propose is that in the GT Keynes wanted to describe *mechanisms* that could explain unemployment instead of raising more revolutionary arguments relying on murkier concepts, such as true uncertainty and its role, in *new* approaches to the workings of entrepreneurial economies. The GT is, to some extent, an essay in persuasion. Keynes refused to engage in debates of a more philosophical nature, trying to connect his theory as much as possible to the classical tradition.[20] Despite Keynes's well known rejection of formal models as an appropriate language to describe complex economic processes, in the GT he made frequent use of them, including in the chapters referred here on liquidity preference. As Kahn pointed out:

> Sufficient has been said to demonstrate the unsuitability of thinking of a schedule of liquidity preference as though it could be represented by a well-defined curve or by a functional relationship expressed in mathematical terms or subject to econometric processes. Keynes himself often gave way to the temptation to picture the state of liquidity preference as a fairly stable relationship, despite his intuitional horror of undue formalism, but this treatment at least can be justified by the need at the time for a forceful and clear-cut exposition if it was to carry any weight at all.
>
> (Kahn 1972: 90)[21]

In this line of reasoning, what Keynes really aimed at in the GT was to show how the interaction between supply of and demand for money could end up determining an interest rate that was too high to allow the investments necessary to reach full employment to be realized.[22] To unclutter the argument, Keynes seems to have decided to shed light on the speculative motive to demand money, whereby the *interest elasticity of money demand* could be established and through which monetary policy is transmitted. This meant minimizing the more revolutionary elements of his theory, the demand for money as a defense against uncertainty and the effect of changes in the state of confidence on money demand and the interest rate. It is possible, however, that the realization that classically-trained readers were not convinced by his argument led Keynes to the more radical stance proposed in 1937.

A deviation from the more conventional treatment of Chapters 13 to 15, of course, is the approach offered in Chapter 17, on the essential properties of interest and money, a chapter long neglected by most readers of the GT. In that chapter, the essential attribute of money is its liquidity premium, that is, the value of "the power of disposal over an asset during a period [which] may offer a potential convenience or security" to its holder (CW 7: 226).[23] Every asset may offer a liquidity premium, but money not only "pays" the highest liquidity premium of all assets in a monetary economy, but it is also the only asset for which "its liquidity-premium much exceeds its carrying cost" (CW 7: 227), which means that it is the only asset that can actually satisfy a precautionary demand as defined by Keynes. A large part of Chapter 17 is then dedicated to the identification of elements that confer this property on money, some of them connected to its state of permanent relative scarcity (the negligible production and substitution elasticities), others connected to its demand (being the asset in which debts are denominated and liquidated (CW 7: 233ff.).

Summary of the argument

There seems to be a significant gap between the approaches offered by Keynes in the GT itself and his defense of the GT against its critics in 1937. The GT clearly emphasizes the speculative demand for money, while the 1937 paper focuses on factors like confidence, and the role of money as a protective device against unpredictable adverse events.[24] But the theory offered in the chapters on liquidity preference in the GT is not unfortunate just because it conceals what Keynes later declared to be essential. It was particularly unfortunate in that *concealment was done by merging the innovative element, the precautionary demand, with the most traditional of monetary theories, the quantitative theory of money*, the validity of which is confined precisely to the transactions demand for money.

The explanation for the dissonance that is proposed in this chapter relies on Keynes's desire to convey the notion that, for a given state of long-term expectations, involuntary unemployment was caused by a divergence between actual interest rates and the rate of interest that would support full employment. The latter should be equal to the marginal efficiency of capital for a volume of investment equal to full employment savings. Keynes seemed to give priority to describing the mechanisms through which this divergence could emerge and last for indefinitely long periods, instead of digging into its deeper causes, a priority he seemed to have abandoned in the 1937 paper.

An important result of these choices, however, was that while the two-types-of-motive reduced from the three-motives scheme of the GT became universally known as "the" Keynesian theory of money demand[25], the deeper discussion of 1937 was largely ignored by economist readers, in much the same way that Keynes's debate with Ohlin on the relation between savings, investment and the interest rate was also neglected. Keynes's monetary theory in the GT then became the target of friendly and not so friendly critics for some flaws that can be traced to the problems identified in this section. In the rest of this chapter we discuss two among the most important of these criticisms. First, we examine Kahn's and afterwards Tobin's reconstructions of Keynes's theory, both concerned with the same problem: how Keynes dealt with uncertainty in the chapters of the GT on liquidity preference.

3   Richard Kahn's "Some Notes on Liquidity Preference"[26]

Both Kahn and Tobin objected (the second implicitly, as we will see in the next section) to Keynes's grouping of motives to demand money, merging the precautionary demand into the transactions demand for money, on the one hand, and the speculative demand on the other. Kahn, however, agreed with Keynes that the interest elasticity of the demand for money function is due to the operation of the speculative motive, while Tobin tried to root the sensitivity of money demand to interest rate changes in a modified form of the precautionary demand.

According to Kahn, it is difficult to separate the precautionary from the speculative motives since both deal with inactive balances, where money is held as an asset instead of a means of payment held in anticipation of planned expenditures.[27] The difference between them, Kahn proposed, has to do with uncertainty:

> But in principle the precautionary motive can be said to operate in so far as some persons think that the rate of interest is likely to move; the speculative motive in so far as some persons think that on balance it is likely to move one way rather than the other.
>
> (Kahn 1972: 81)

In other words, the precautionary demand has to do with the *possibility of change*, while the speculative motive is a bet on a *certain direction of change*. Kahn's own approach was to make the speculative demand for money a definite bet on the direction of change in future interest rates, to be affected by the confidence with which the wealth holder entertains this expectation of change. Thus, "what the precautionary motive does is to give the speculative motive something to bite on" (Kahn, 1972: 87).

As a matter of fact, Kahn criticized Keynes's absolute separation between the two motives precisely because it prevented him from considering the influence of *conviction* on speculative demand decisions (Kahn, 1972: 88). His own solution was to consider that "[h]ow far [a] person gives way to the operation of the speculative motive depends on the extent of his feeling of risk and uncertainty about the behavior of the rate of interest" (Kahn, 1972: 82). But the influence of conviction, or confidence, to use one of Keynes's own terms, on the demand for inactive balances works through the precautionary demand for money. According to Kahn, the influence of the degree of conviction on the operation of the speculative demand for money, therefore, "demonstrates how impossible it is to identify the quantity of money held on account of the speculative motive. The two motives do not act additively: the demand for money is a complicated outcome of their interplay" (Kahn, 1972: 85).

Kahn suggested, in fact, that the situation may be even more complicated because different groups of people face different sources of uncertainty in different degrees:

> At the one extreme is the feeling of *income risk*, at the other extreme the feeling of *capital risk*. It is more picturesque than accurate to associate income risk particularly with widows and orphans, and while the feeling of capital risk is experienced particularly by financial institutions, it in fact applies very widely.
>
> (Kahn 1972: 82)

The distinction is relevant, according to Kahn, because if income risk is more important for a given group of people than capital risk, there will also emerge a precautionary demand for securities rather than for money when uncertainty rises. Thus, contrary to what Keynes suggested, the demand for money may not be a precise barometer of distrust under all conceivable circumstances.

The simultaneous consideration of the precautionary and the speculative motives and of income and capital risks avoids the weaknesses of Keynes's approach in the GT at the cost of a considerable increase in the complexity of the theory. Now definite results can only be obtained after specifying the larger number of elements that define each possible class of outcomes. Some previously unknown constraints emerge, like the need to specify values for the degrees of bearishness or bullishness and the importance of income or capital risk to determine the final impact of an increase in uncertainty over the demand for securities and money.

The general gist of Kahn's solution, however, can be simply stated and seems to be more in line with Keynes's restatement of priorities in 1937 than the presentation in the GT. We can summarize it in two propositions. First, it is a mistake to conflate the transactions and the precautionary demands into one liquidity function having income as the independent variable. The precautionary demand for money has much more in common with the speculative demand for money, not only because they are both forms of inactive balances but, mostly, because they both relate to modalities of holding wealth through time. The inter-action between the precautionary and speculative demands, in addition, avoids the trap of predicting specialized portfolios (in money or in securities) as the result of the operation solely of the speculative demand for money.

Second, acknowledging a fundamental interrelation between the precaution-ary and the speculative demands does not invalidate the idea that the interest elasticity of money demand is explained by the latter. The precautionary demand, in the interest rate/money quantity space determines the *position* of the curve (jointly with the transactions demand). However, the position does not depend solely on the level of income, but also on the state of confidence on expectations, as defined by Keynes in the GT (CW 7: 148). Therefore, *variations in the perceived level of uncertainty displace the liquidity preference schedule in the interest rate/money quantity space up or downwards*. Reconstructed in this way, the motives-to-demand-money model of the GT can be easily reconciled with Keynes's 1937 statements, according to which changes in the rate of interest may result from changes in the state of confidence (or in the perceived level of uncertainty, which is the same thing) for a given money supply or from changes in money supply for a given state of confidence.[28]

4 James Tobin's "Liquidity Preference as Behavior Towards Risk"[29]

Tobin, like Kahn and, in fact many other critics of Keynes's presentation of liquidity preference in the GT, also took issue with one result of the operation of the speculative demand for money: the specialization of portfolios of bulls (all in securities) and bears (all in money). The aggregate portfolio would still contain money and securities, but each individual investor would either demand solely securities or money.

According to Tobin, this counterfactual result was due to the unusual form of uncertainty that Keynes postulated in the chapters of the GT dedicated to liquidity preference. According to Tobin, "[w]hen [Keynes] refers to uncertainty in the market, he appears to mean disagreement among investors concerning the future of the rate of interest rather than the subjective doubt in the mind of an individual investor" (Tobin, 1987: 248)

The main implication of this particular (and peculiar) notion of uncertainty, that we called "systemic," would be the possibility that rational investors could entertain different evaluations as to the *normal* level of the rate of interest while none of them would be wrong *a priori*. The normal rate of interest was not sup-posed to be determined by objective forces (or by *fundamentals*, as the term became popular nowadays). It would be objectively indeterminate so that each individual investor could, based on his own experience and judgment of what was relevant, evaluate by himself what its value was.[30] Tobin's criticism is the same as that raised by Kahn when he argued that Keynes's focus on the specula-tive demand did not leave any room for the influence of confidence or degrees of conviction on the portfolio choice decision.

Tobin's aims with his article were two-fold: (i) to offer an alternative model of the demand for money that preserved its sensitivity to interest rate changes; and (ii) to explain why individual investors would hold diversified portfolios in terms of money and securities. To achieve both results, Tobin explicitly reintroduced a form of precautionary demand in his scheme, that is, the demand for money as a result of perceived uncertainty. In a sense, Tobin sets himself a similar task to Kahn's, to construct a theory of money demand where one cannot tell which part of money holdings is due to precaution and which one is due to speculation with the future price of securities.

The way Tobin did it was to model explicitly the effects of introducing uncertainty in the portfolio choice. Differently from Keynes's 1937 wider concept, though, uncertainty was modeled as the (calculable) risk of changes in the prices of securities, measured by the variance of the distribution of probabilities of future capital gains.

The model is simple. Tobin assumed the existence of two assets, riskless (and yieldless) money and a risky security, a perpetuity, which offers two types of returns: interest income at a rate r, and capital gains g. Capital gains, which depend on future interest rates, are assumed to be normally distributed with zero mean and variance σ_g. The total return of a portfolio depends on the proportion in which it is allocated to securities (A_1 to money, A_2 in securities, $A_1 + A_2 = 1$). Under these conditions, the expected return of the portfolio is given by:

$$E(R) = A_2 r = \mu_R \tag{1}$$

Portfolio risk is given by:

$$\sigma_R = A_2 \sigma_g \tag{2}$$

From equations (1) and (2), one obtains:

$$\mu_R = \sigma_R (r / \sigma_g) \tag{3}$$

For a given interest rate r and a given variance of capital gains distribution σ_g, average returns, μ_R, are an increasing function of the variance of the total portfolio, σ_R. Total portfolio risk, on the other hand, is a function of A_2, the proportion that is dedicated to securities.

Equation (3) works as a "budget constraint" in Tobin's model. It describes how much risk an individual investor has to accept in order to pursue a given expected rate of return. Which combination of risk and return will be actually chosen will depend on the risk preferences of each investor. Tobin draws indifference curves to reflect those preferences and obtains the two results he desired, a demand for money function that is sensitive to interest rates (and with the right sign) and individual investor's portfolios that are diversified, containing both money and securities.[31]

Unfortunately, as Tobin promptly admitted, these neat results are entirely dependent on the specific shape and position of the indifference curves between risk and return one selects. The graphical solution presented by Tobin is, in fact, more of an illustration of a *possible* result than a proof developed from stated premises. In fact, Tobin shows that even risk prone investors can reach equilibrium solutions that show sensitivity to interest rates, but with the wrong sign. Perhaps even more worrisome, a special category of risk averters, which Tobin called "plungers," would seek corner solutions, with specialized portfolios. To achieve general results one would have to be able to place additional, possibly ad hoc constraints on indifference curves, which, Tobin acknowledged, could be awkward to justify.

Thus, as Kahn before him, Tobin also failed in his attempt to construct a model in which the explicit consideration of uncertainty could fully explain diversification of portfolios at the same time in which a significant degree of interest elasticity of money demand was preserved under more or less general conditions. Other constraints have to be added for the model to offer more definite theoretical predictions.

Interestingly, both papers seem to share the assumption that one does not need to take into consideration Keynes's strong view of uncertainty to explain the behavior of the demand for money.[32] This is, of course, explicit in Tobin's approach but, perhaps more surprisingly, Kahn also made clear in his paper that "the words "risk" and "uncertainty" are used in the conventional manner as indicating the degree of dispersion of the probability distribution, and the reliability of the probability distribution" (Kahn 1972: 81fn). Still, the central message of both papers, that the precautionary demand for money is the key channel to relate money demand and uncertainty, seems to survive this limitation. First, it was by no means obvious in the 1950s that dispersion of results could not be taken as a proper measure of uncertainty, since the latter, in a sense, means precisely that one cannot know what is going to happen because a lot of things can actually happen in the future. Frank Hahn's demonstration that calculable probabilities would eliminate the need for money, mentioned in footnote 6 of this chapter, above, was still a long time ahead. Particularly in the case of Kahn's paper, one should notice the reference to the *reliability* of the probability distribution. What did he possibly mean by that? Only under true uncertainty there is room for concern with reliability, another word, in fact, for confidence.

In addition, both Tobin and Kahn discuss the demand for money assuming a different aggregative structure than the one used in the GT. Keynes clarified in its Chapter 13 (CW 7: 167fn) that he considered two assets in his liquidity preference model: *money* and *debts*.[33] In such a model, of course, there can be only one interest rate: "the" interest rate. The interest rate paid on "the" bond will compensate for all the *moneyness* elements lacking in bonds, including uncertainty in all of its meanings. Tobin and Kahn, in contrast, deal explicitly with short-term interest rates, paid on the immediate money substitutes, like short-term debt. Kahn explicitly mentions that he was dealing with repetitive, largely reversible movements in the prices of securities, not with investments, assuming that in the case of securities prices "the concept of a probability distribution is perhaps less unhappily applied to expectations" (Kahn 1972: 81fn). In fact,

Keynes himself did something similar in his treatment of short-term expectations in Chapter 5 of the GT.

In any case, the formal modeling of probability distributions by Tobin had a much stronger influence on the literature than Kahn's vaguer references to them. One could perhaps suggest the hypothesis that it may have been precisely the reason why Tobin's 1958 paper, written to defend an important proposition of Keynesianism, in the debate against monetarism, that money demand is interest-elastic, ended up fathering anti-Keynesian models of capital asset pricing.

5 Conclusion: why should we care?

One may see this whole discussion as just another curiosum, an arcane game of words and labels to entertain hagiographers of Keynes. In fact, it is not. Generations of economists have been trained in macro and monetary economics through the use of money demand and supply models where stable relations between money demand and its determinants, income and interest rates, are assumed by construction. Anybody whose macroeconomics training was based on the use of IS/LM models never actually heard about the ways in which perceived uncertainty can affect the demand for money, and, through that, the level of interest rates. The shifts in the liquidity preference schedule that have been so important in shaping the financial crisis of 2007–2008, and its aftermath, cannot be explained by these models.[34]

There are four essential implications of the correct identification of the roles of the three motives to demand money:

1   As both Kahn and Tobin insisted, the traditional analysis of the transactions and the speculative motives, which seems to closely correspond to what Keynes actually proposed in the GT, misses the role of variables such as conviction or confidence, which are important only when one considers that agents *feel* uncertain about their expectations about the future. A byproduct of this limitation is the empirically false proposition that individual portfolios of bears and bulls should be fully specialized in holding either securities or money.

2   The stability of the liquidity preference schedule (or the money demand function) is overestimated in the formulation offered by Keynes in the GT. Shifts of the function are assumed to result only of changes in income levels, which cause variations in the transactions demand. This contrasts with the stress on the fragility of such functions proposed by Keynes in 1937, which authors close to him, like Kahn, insisted on being an essential element of his theoretical approach.

3   Connected with the preceding argument, one important implication of properly considering the relation between changes in the degree of confidence and shifts in the liquidity preference schedule is the realization that the impact of monetary policy may be less predictable in moments of increased uncertainty, during, for instance, financial crises. In these periods, while

monetary policy may still induce movements *along* the liquidity preference function, this effect may be overwhelmed by a *shift* in the function itself caused by an increase in uncertainty. Besides, both Kahn and Tobin pointed out that the shape of the precautionary demand function may be more complex than one may think at first, either because of possibly different sensitivities to classes of threats (Kahn's argument) or by differences in risk aversion (Tobin's argument).

4   Finally, the proper understanding of why money can ultimately satisfy a precautionary demand for safer assets may shed light on the properties of liquidity itself and why, in moments of stronger stress, the monetary liabilities of monetary authorities, that is, the money created by the State, may become the choice asset of the economy. During normal times, privately-issued become substitutes for currency as liquidity vehicles. During crises, however, the same private liabilities tend to be rejected and a flight to the safety of public debt and currency takes place. Why this is so can be better understood when one explicitly considers the role of uncertainty and confidence in the process of wealth accumulation.

Neither Kahn, nor Tobin referred to Keynes's 1937 paper when they revisited liquidity preference theory, even though Kahn at least was familiar with it, having sent comments to Keynes after reading it still in manuscript. Both Kahn and Tobin seemed to have shared the same view as to the shortcomings of Keynes's presentation in the GT. Between them, Kahn's proposal seems to be the closest to Keynes's formulation. He articulated the two motives that recognized money as a form of wealth which allowed him to identify the influence of monetary policy through the speculative demand and of the state of confidence through the precautionary motive.

It seems inevitable to conclude that Keynes's arguments when presenting liquidity preference theory in the GT were flawed. It should be noticed, however, that Keynes himself warned against taking them too literally. As he wrote in 1937:

> I am more attached to the comparatively simple fundamental ideas which underlie my theory than to the particular forms in which I have embodied them, and I have no desire that the latter should be crystallized at the present stage of the debate.
>
> (CW 14: 111)

The determinants of money demand have always been of central concern to Keynesian economics, in all of its strands.[35] Tobin's model became the foundation on which most of the monetary theory associated with American Keynesianism (or neoclassical synthesis, as Paul Samuelson called it). Kahn's paper is an important piece in the Cambridge legacy, which led to parallel developments to those of American Keynesianism. This book is clearly associated with this second tradition.

Notes

1 The second was the consumption multiplier. We will not be concerned in this chapter with the multiplier, a concept that generated its own heated controversy through the years, even among committed Keynesians. It will be treated later, however, in Chapter 6.

2 Leontieff focused his criticism on the speculative demand for money, arguing that it was based on differences between expected and realized values for the rate of interest, which should disappear in equilibrium situations. In this case, in equilibrium, Keynes's money demand function would collapse to a traditional Marhallian quantitative theory of money and only the fancy new labels would remain.

3 This section is an exploration of the article "The General Theory of Employment," published originally in *The Quarterly Journal of Economics*, February 1937. The quotations, however, are taken from its reprint in *The Collected Writings of John Maynard Keynes*, volume 14, here referred, as with other volumes in the collection for this book's purposes as CW 14.

4 A distinctive characteristic of any variant of the Keynesian theory of expectations is the recognition of the importance not only of estimating the future behavior of the relevant variables but also of assessing the degree of confidence the decision-maker has on her estimates. The present author has discussed Keynes's concepts of probability and uncertainty in Chapter 4 of Cardim de Carvalho (1992), an approach strongly influenced by G.L.S. Shackle's writings. See also Runde (1994) for a similar view.

5 "I accuse the classical economic theory of being itself one of these pretty, polite techniques which tries to deal with the present by abstracting from the fact that we know very little about the future" (CW 14: 115).

6 See, for instance, Hahn (1984), Chapter 7. Hahn criticizes Patinkin in that chapter showing that any payment process that can be reduced to calculable probabilities preserve the fundamental neutrality of money and therefore do not interfere with assumed intrinsic tendencies toward full employment.

7

> Money ... is a store of wealth. So we are told, without a smile on the face. But in the world of the classical economy, that an insane use to which to put it! For it is a recognized characteristic of money as a store of wealth that it is barren; whereas practically every other form of storing wealth yields some interest or profit.
>
> (CW 14: 115)

8 Any commercial transaction in a market economy involves the creation of a contractual obligation, even when no formal document has been signed. Market transactions are always bilateral so that the completion of one leg of it implies the obligation for the parts to complete the operation by performing the complementary act. Whether a formal document is signed or not is a detail, depending on the cost of formalizing the operation compared to its actual value.

9 As some authors such as Paul Davidson and Hyman Minsky have added, it is so, especially if the agent had issued debts in the past that are outstanding in the present.

10 Otherwise, calculations of probabilities is reduced to a mere mathematical operation, about which there is no room for trust or distrust.

11 It is the conscience that the basis for calculations is precarious that makes confidence so important.

> The state of long-term expectation, upon which our decisions are based, does not solely depend, therefore, on the most probable forecast we can make. It also depends on the *confidence* with which we make this forecast – on how highly we rate the likelihood of our best forecast turning out quite wrong.... The outstanding fact is the extreme precariousness of the basis of knowledge on which our

estimates of prospective yield have to be made. Our knowledge of the factors which will govern the yield of an investment some years hence is usually vey slight and often negligible. If we speak frankly, we have to admit that our basis of knowledge for estimating the yield ten years hence of a railway, a copper mine, a textile factory, the goodwill of a patent medicine, an Atlantic liner, a building in the City of London amounts to little and sometimes to nothing; or even five years hence.

(CW 7: 148–150)

12 See Chapter 4, below, for an examination of Keynes views on the determination of the money supply.

13 For a discussion of the relationship between saving and investment, a point where the opposition between Keynes and the classics has been frequently misunderstood, see Chapter 6, below.

14 See Chapter 3, below.

15 As Hicks (1967: 15–16) pointed out, however, it may not be appropriate to classify the transactions motive as a reason to "demand" money, since the demand for money in this context "is just the indirect consequence of decisions taken for quite other reasons, with no direct calculations of their monetary repercussions." On the other hand, as to the precautionary and speculative motives "the notion of a voluntary demand for money is unquestionably appropriate" (Hicks 1967: 17). In any case, agents do retain money in anticipation of purchases of goods and services affecting the amount of money in circulation left to satisfy the "authentic" demand for money, affecting thereby the interest rate as well.

16 Tobin will also stress the point but apparently he neglected the fact that Keynes referred to both senses.

17 As Keynes himself recognized, in the absence of a precautionary demand for money, if the speculative demand for money happens to be zero (that is, in a situation where prevails the expectation that current interest rates will continue in the future), his liquidity function will reduce to the quantity theory of money (CW 7: 209).

18 This equation contributed to strengthen the perception of stability of the money demand function. Usually plotted as a descending curve in interest rate/quantity of money space, it is assumed that once the level of income, Y, is given, the position of the function is determined, since $L_1(Y)$ becomes the intercept of the function. The impact of changes in the perceived degree of uncertainty (and, thus, of confidence) is therefore lost, even as a shift factor.

19 And one should keep in mind that *definite* expectations are not the same thing as *correct* expectations. In fact, both bears and bulls are assumed to hold definite expectations, but of course both groups cannot hold correct expectations at the same time.

20 That the GT was an attempt to persuade the community of economists, where the overwhelming majority of members shared (and still do) classical views, can also be surmised by the successive changes in the intended structure of the book, as Keynes recorded them in the planned tables of contents he prepared for its several drafts. As documented in volumes 13 and 29 of his Collected Writings, the GT was originally conceived to be presented as a direct and frontal challenge to the classical tradition, arguing that classical economists focused on the wrong type of economy, a *cooperative* economy, while Keynes focused on *entrepreneurial*, or *monetary*, economies. In the first tables of contents prepared by Keynes, the challenge was to be put right away in Chapter 1, dedicated to the concept of monetary economy. In the published work, this fundamental challenge was replaced by much milder statements about the validity of specific postulates of classical theory and of the adequacy of classical theory for a specific type, but not for the generality of types, of market economies.

21 Uncertainty and confidence were not only new variables challenging conventional wisdom. They were also difficult concepts to define formally and empirically.

Keynes's own approach was somewhat vague: "[t]here is, however, not much to be said about the state of confidence *a priori*. Our conclusions must mainly depend upon the actual observation of markets and business psychology (CW 7: 149).

22

> The difficulties in the way of maintaining effective demand at a level high enough to provide full employment, which ensue from the association of a conventional and fairly stable long-term rate of interest with a fickle and highly unstable marginal efficiency of capital, should be, by now, obvious to the reader.
>
> (CW 7: 204)

23 Much more on this will be proposed in the next chapters, especially Chapter 4.

24 In more formalistic terms, the GT stresses factors explaining the *inclination* of the liquidity preference schedule, while in 1937 Keynes focused on its *position*.

25 By being absorbed, for instance, in canonical models like the IS/LM family of models, which became inextricably associated with Keynesian theory.

26 Kahn's paper was published originally in *The Manchester School*, 1954. References in this chapter were taken from its reprint in *Selected Essays on Employment and Growth* (Kahn 1972).

27 Even though, in a sense, the speculative motive shares with the transactions motive the nature of being demand for money to acquire something definite, not demand for money as such, as Hicks suggested. In the first case, it is demand for money in anticipation of an asset purchase, whereas in the latter it is to acquire a good or service. The speculative demand is a class of inactive balances only with respect to goods, but it is demand for money as a means of payment in a planned transaction. On the other hand, differently from the transactions demand, spending money held for speculative reasons is not constrained by contractual clauses, so its "velocity" may be much harder to pin down.

28 At the end of the day, in the GT Keynes seemed more interested in relating the interest rate to monetary policy, while in the 1937 article he seemed more interested in relating it to uncertainty. But there is no necessary contradiction between the two objectives once the determinants of the liquidity preference schedule are properly presented.

29 Tobin's "Liquidity Preference as Behavior Towards Risk" was originally published in the *Review of Economic Studies*, in 1958. The quotations are taken from its reprint in his *Essays in Economics*, vol. I (Tobin 1987).

30 One should remember that Keynes in the GT explicitly rejected both Fisher's and Wicksell's theories of the rate of interest.

31 The visual representation of the equilibrium to such a model is familiar to every student of monetary economics. See Tobin (1987: 250).

32 Bibow (1998: 260) argues that Tobin was justified in employing the concept of risk since in his model the distinction between uncertainty and risk did not matter "in terms of their economic effects."

33 Leijonhufvud (1968) showed that, except for a few occasions, like Chapter 17, Keynes used a dichotomous aggregative structure throughout the GT.

34 The importance of such movements of the liquidity preference schedule will be explored in Chapter 9, below.

35 Cardim de Carvalho (1995) presented the central lines of development of the post Keynesian approach to liquidity preference. Bibow (1998) offered a very instructive discussion of some developments of liquidity preference theory, giving particular prominence to Hicks and Tobin.

3 Liquidity premium, liquidity risk and liquidity preference

1 Introduction

A common thread running through all the chapters in this book is that liquidity preference theory, as advanced in the GT and Keynes's other publications of the time, is in fact a theory of asset pricing, an essential foundation for a theory of the drivers of capital accumulation in a modern entrepreneurial economy.[1]

In a nutshell, liquidity preference theory states that the *demand* price of an asset, that is, the price a buyer offers to acquire a given asset, is the present value of the revenues the buyer expects to earn from the possession of the said asset plus its liquidity premium, that is, the margin the asset buyer is prepared to pay above the value of expected revenues in exchange for the ability the asset is expected to yield its owner to sell it to other buyers quickly and without significant loss.[2] The more liquid an asset is, that is, the higher its liquidity premium, the less expected revenues potential buyers demand to acquire it. In the case of the most liquid of assets, money, asset holders are usually prepared to give up any earnings to keep it in their portfolios. Since the notion of production cost is foreign to financial assets, including money, *equilibrium* prices are mostly determined by demand prices.

Keynes formalized his theory of asset pricing in Chapter 17 of *The General Theory*, through the concept of own-rates of interest.[3] Every asset is expected to yield some revenue, either as income (profits, dividends, interest, rents, etc.) or as capital gain (the difference between the purchase and the sale prices, which can very well be negative, if the sale price of the asset is below the price paid for it). On the other hand, holding assets may impose some cost on their holders, no matter what they choose to do with them, using them or keeping them idle. Keynes called the incomes generated by an asset, net of costs incurred in its utilization, *quasi-rents*, denoted by q.[4] Capital gains were denoted by a (for capital appreciation or depreciation). Carrying costs, that is, the costs incurred by simply holding the asset, were called c. Therefore, an asset is supposed to yield money revenues to the rate of $a + q - c$. However, these are *expected* values, conditional on some expected future development actually taking place. But inhabitants of the world described by Keynes know that their expectations may go wrong in many ways, including some which they cannot even conceive or describe *a priori* so that no efficient hedge instrument can be devised to neutralize them.[5] That is where liquidity comes in. The asset buyer is reassured if the asset can be expected to be sold in the case of the future turning out to be substantially different from what was expected when the asset was purchased. If and when the buyer comes to realize that she made a wrong move, she can zero the game simply by selling the asset to others if the asset is liquid. If the buyer can be reassured about the possibility of placing the asset back in the market without significant losses, she will accept a "discount" in the expected revenues to be earned by buying it. Keynes actually inverted the reasoning to state that if an asset is less than perfectly liquid, its buyer will demand a reward for its relative illiquidity. This reward is the rate of interest paid by the asset. Liquidity, therefore, acts as kind of general insurance policy to "lull the buyer's disquietude."[6]

In sum, liquidity preference theory states that in order to attract holders assets have to offer prospective money revenues that are proportional to their perceived illiquidity, that is, its exposure to liquidity risks. LP theory privileges, therefore, liquidity risks in the explanation of how asset prices are determined. But what about other risks? Don't they affect asset prices? Aren't they plagued too by the same fundamental uncertainties that shape liquidity risk?

Keynes's almost exclusive focus on liquidity risk in the GT may be understood in two ways. One possible interpretation is that, as he had announced a few years before the publication of that book, Keynes's goal was to establish the distinctive features of a *monetary economy* (or a *monetary production economy*, as he first called it) to contrast them with the notion of "cooperative" economy which he associated with what he called "classical" economics. One does not need too much economic theory to accept the intuitive notion that liquidity is the principal, or perhaps the only one, attribute of *money as an asset* and is the main reason why wealth holders keep resources in money form in their portfolios even though they generally don't generate any revenues. In this line of argument, if Keynes had believed that, for instance, the main distinctive feature of modern economies was that capitalists were responsible for productive investments, it would be the investment risks that would have been selected for examination, leaving the others to the footnotes.

An alternative interpretation, however, is that, in Keynes's view, liquidity is *not* an attribute like the others and liquidity risk is not just a particular class of risks so that a more general theory of asset pricing should explicitly consider all the other risks involved in wealth accumulation. It is arguable, in fact, that liquidity risk (and liquidity premium, for that matter) occupies a special place in Keynes *vision* of how an entrepreneurial economy works and it is because of its liquidity attribute that money plays a special role in his theoretical framework. In the rest of this chapter, we will examine liquidity preference under each of these two interpretations to try and decide why liquidity risks were given such a large amount of attention by Keynes in comparison with other classes of risk.

2 Liquidity premium narrowly considered

Liquidity premium is introduced by Keynes in *The General Theory* as follows:

> Finally, the power of disposal over an asset during a period may offer a
> potential convenience or security, which is not equal for assets of different
> kinds, though the assets themselves are of equal initial value. There is, so to
> speak, nothing to show for this at the end of the period in the shape of
> output; yet it is something for which people are ready to pay something. The
> amount ... which they are willing to pay for the potential convenience or
> security given by this power of disposal (exclusive of yield or carrying cost
> attaching to the asset), we shall call its liquidity-premium *l*.
>
> (CW 7: 226)

Liquidity is, thus, defined as "the power of disposal over an asset during a
period." The very compact definition may conceal the complexity of the liquidity
attribute. Keynes seems to rely on an intuitive understanding of the notion of
liquidity on the part of his readers so that such a description should be enough to
convey that complexity.

The power of disposal over an asset encompasses at least two dimensions. All
else being equal, the quicker one can sell that asset, the more liquid it is. But any
asset can be sold very quickly if its holder is willing to accept unlimited losses
from that trade. So another dimension is, all else being the same, the more a
given asset can conserve its value when its holder decides to sell it, the more
liquid it is. The asset holder, however, may have to hold on to that asset for an
indefinitely long period of time while she waits for some prospective buyer to
emerge who will offer a price which she judges fair. Common usage, as that on
which Keynes seemed to rely when giving his definition, would hold that
liquidity, therefore, is a bi-dimensional phenomenon: an asset is liquid when one
can expect to sell it quickly, with minimal losses, if any.

The key factor to determine the liquidity of an asset is the existence of deep,
permanent, and organized secondary markets for that item.[7] More abstractly, to
assume that an asset is liquid it is necessary to believe that there will be an
excess *reservation demand* for that asset at all times. Liquid assets must be
scarce in the economic sense of the world, that is, its supply must be smaller
than demand at current and expected prices. Keynes argued that it was the existence of limits on the supply of those assets that guaranteed that these markets
would be always characterized by positive excess demands.[8] Limited supply,
however, is a necessary but not sufficient condition for liquidity. Liquidity
premia are only significant in the case of assets traded in *organized* markets, the
existence of which reduces transaction costs to a minimum.

Formally, *illiquidity risk* is the risk of being unable to sell an asset or to sell
without suffering significant losses. One may think, in some extreme cases, of an
absolute illiquidity risk, a situation where an asset "turns into dust" because
nobody wants to buy them at any price.[9] More commonly, this notion of

liquidity, that some economists call *market liquidity*, is measured by the fall in price expected to be needed for the market to absorb a given amount of the asset under consideration.

Market liquidity, however, does not exhaust the meaning of liquidity. In fact, more generally, we may think of liquidity as the ability of an asset to give its owner access to money.[10] Such access may be obtained by selling the asset, as in the concept of market liquidity stressed by Keynes in Chapter 17 of the GT. But it may also be obtained by borrowing against assets which are acceptable as collateral (as in repurchase operations, for instance). In fact, one could think of pre-contracted credit lines as a source of liquidity in this sense. Thinking of liquidity of the *whole balance sheet* instead of just considering the liquidity of assets marked the main contribution of Hyman Minsky to develop Keynes's pioneering approach to this notion.

Minsky's central concern was focused on one's ability to honor one's debts when they fell due. There are many ways to ensure it. First, one could match assets and liabilities in a way to reconcile cash in- and out-flows to minimize illiquidity risks in the form of an inability to honor one's debts when they come due. One could call it *balance sheet liquidity* and it can be strengthened to the extent in which the wealth holder observes sufficient safety margins between expected returns and committed payments. A second way is to keep a certain proportion of one's assets in money and other highly liquid assets, such as Treasury bills. Highly liquid assets are easily accepted as collaterals in short-term loans, creating thus a third channel to access money. Finally, contingent and other pre-arranged credit lines also reinforce one's ability to pay debts even when expectations of asset revenues are disappointed for any reason.

It should be clear, however, that, as important as liquidity (or illiquidity) risk may be in a modern entrepreneurial economy, it could hardly be seen as the only class of risks that should affect asset prices. One can easily think of other important classes of risks, and in fact in several passages of The GT and of other contemporary works Keynes did refer to them. In particular, one could think that in the case of "widows and orphans," for instance, those classes of wealth holders that intend to keep assets to maturity, illiquidity risk would be at most a minor consideration for them when forming their demand prices in comparison to, say, credit risk. Other risks should probably more strongly contribute to the formation of these prices.

3 Other risks

If one takes liquidity risk in its narrow sense, that is, the risk of not being able to access cash quickly when needed, or in its even narrower sense of not being able to sell an asset quickly, at a price that does not impose significant losses on its holder, it is not self-evident that this type of risk may have any claim of priority over other classes of risk. In fact, many, perhaps most, present day Keynesians, if asked, would probably say that the main class of risks affecting economic activity is profit risk, the risk evaluated by entrepreneurs that they may not get the profits that could justify an investment. Profit expectations may be frustrated for many reasons, and it is certainly important to know the most important causes for such frustration,[11] but what matters for entrepreneurs is certainly the bottom line: how should they evaluate the possibility of not getting the profits that would make a project worthwhile.

Keynes did dedicate much attention to the formation of profit expectations, both in his discussion of short and long term expectations, in Chapter 5, and in the discussions of the inducements to investment, in Chapters 11 and 12 of the GT. It was with respect to the long term expectations that orient decisions to invest that Keynes introduced some of his most important ideas about how uncertainty shapes not only individual behaviors (as in the case of the notion of *conventional behavior*) but also institutions (such as Stock Exchanges). Nevertheless, these concerns are not carried on to the discussion of how prices of assets are formed, in Chapter 17. In fact, in that chapter, the variable "q", the rate of quasi-rents, of which profits are a particular item, is defined without any special remark about the fundamental uncertainty that surrounds its calculation. The essence of the concept was introduced before, in Chapter 11, on the notion of marginal efficiency of capital, where its expectational nature is emphasized. However, the stress on expectations in the latter discussion only serves the purpose of allowing Keynes to criticize the concept of marginal productivity of capital: while the former covers expected revenues throughout the life of the investment, the latter reflected only current conditions. No considerations on how risks are included in these expectations are offered.

One has to go back to the first pages of the GT to find out how Keynes disposed of the issue. There, he stated that the level of employment "depends on the amount of the proceeds which the entrepreneurs expect to receive from the corresponding output." At this point Keynes explained in a footnote:

> An entrepreneur, who has to reach a practical decision as to his scale of production, does not, of course, entertain a single undoubting expectation of what the sale-proceeds of a given output will be, but several hypothetical expectations held with varying degrees of probability and definiteness. By his expectation of proceeds I mean, therefore, *that expectation of proceeds which, if it were held with certainty, would lead to the same behavior as does the bundle of vague and more various possibilities which actually makes up his state of expectations when he reaches his decision.*
>
> (CW 7: 24, my emphasis)

The appeal to certainty-equivalents is certainly surprising. If the statement is taken at its face-value, Keynes suggests that profits are not surrounded by the fundamental uncertainty he would describe in his 1937 response to critics, but by calculable risks. The calculation of certainty-equivalents relies on the possibility of knowing not only all "the several hypothetical expectations" of profit but also, as Keynes admits, its "degrees of probabilities". It is very difficult to see how to reconcile this proposition with the 1937 proposition that capital accumulation was the main activity to suffer from the burden of fundamental uncertainty.

The same would apply to other classes of risk, like credit risk. Credit risk is mentioned in the GT when the notion of *lender's risk* is introduced. Keynes approaches the notion, however, as mostly a duplication of the intrinsic risks of enterprise, almost an imperfection resulting from the differentiation of borrowers and lenders:

> [lender's risk] would not exist if the borrower and lender were the same person. Moreover, it involves in part a duplication of a proportion of the entrepreneur's risk, which is added *twice* to the pure rate of interest to give the minimum prospective yield which will induce the investment. For if a venture is a risky one, the borrower will require a wider margin between his expectation of yield and the rate of interest at which he will think it worth his while to borrow; whilst the very same reason will lead the lender to require a wider margin between what he charges and the pure rate of interest in order to induce him to lend (except where the borrower is so strong and wealthy that he is in a position to offer an exceptional margin of security).
>
> (CW 7: 144–145)

Here, as in other passages in the GT, Keynes seems to assume that there is a relationship between risk and required return (and therefore the value of an asset). However, (1) this relationship does not seem to raise his interest, being either ignored or mentioned without comment or explanation;[12] and (2) when the time comes for an explicit discussion of the formation of asset prices in Chapter 17, Keynes seems to assume that calculations relating risks and returns have been performed for all assets *in advance* of the postulation of a method to determine the prices of assets. Liquidity premia, in contrast, is singled out as a kind of risk allowance, deserving special consideration. Why? As proposed in the introduction to this chapter, if we assume that this distinction was deliberate, it could be explained as a link in a chain of argument directed at showing how money becomes a *real* variable in the description of the workings of an entrepreneurial economy. Being free of liquidity risk is what characterizes money when compared to any other asset. To establish money as an asset, and therefore characterize it as a "real" variable affecting the real value of other variables, it was the liquidity premium that had to be explored as a theoretical innovation.

The aggregation of assets in two groups employed in Chapters 13 to 15, money and bonds, allowed Keynes to propose that bonds pay "the" interest rate to compensate for their illiquidity with respect to money, which is the core of liquidity preference theory of *the* rate of interest. Again, the dual aggregation of assets in bonds and capital goods proposed elsewhere in the GT allowed the definition of equilibrium as the equality between "the" rate of interest (there is only one!) and "the" marginal efficiency of capital.

When the time came to disaggregate assets, Keynes would have been moved by the same motivation: to show how money becomes an asset and competes with other forms of wealth in the eyes of buyers. It is the liquidity premium that makes money an asset and allows it to be compared with other assets. Non-monetary assets, on the other hand, should be differentiated according to many criteria, including the particular types of risk to which they are exposed, but this was not perhaps a question Keynes wanted to explore, since it was not distinctive of a monetary economy. The passages where the relation between risk and return is mentioned should attest that Keynes was not oblivious to it, but his look was focused on money, not on the choice between non-monetary assets.

But this is not the only possible explanation for the singling out of the importance of liquidity attributes in the formation of asset prices.

4 Liquidity premium in a wider sense

In at least one occasion Keynes argued that liquidity premium should not be assimilated to the general category of risk premia:

> The owners of wealth will then weigh the lack of "liquidity" of different capital equipments in the above sense as a medium in which to hold wealth against the best available actuarial estimate of their prospective yields after allowing for risk. *The liquidity-premium, it will be observed, is partly similar to the risk-premium, but partly different; – the difference corresponding to the difference between the best estimates we can make of probabilities and the confidence with which we make them.* When we were dealing … with the estimation of prospective yield, we did not enter into detail as to how the estimation is made: and to avoid complicating the argument, we did not distinguish differences in liquidity from differences in risk proper.
>
> (CW 7: 240, my emphasis)

The similarity is established by the fact that liquidity premium and risk premium are both compensations for the possibility of future losses from the acquisition of a given asset or set of assets. The difference seems to be that risks are established by the probabilities of adverse developments that could frustrate yield expectations while the demand for liquidity and its value in the eyes of asset buyers depend on the latter's confidence that they got their calculations right so that they will not need to depend on other "escape strategies" later.

Thus, the demand for liquidity responds to uncertainty as such, that is, the acknowledgment that prediction (and risk calculations) may not be enough to ensure a proper hedging of the decisions made. If an asset is liquid, whatever the nature of the threat that may come to materialize later, including the possibility that specific risks may have been underestimated at the time of the purchase of the asset, it will always still be possible to find an emergency exit by shifting the asset to someone else.

In this sense, liquidity premia refer to liquidity risk in an ample sense. Whatever may go wrong (disappointment of profit or dividend expectations, disappointment of capital appreciation expectations, defaults by borrowers, operational problems, and so on) in the future, if an asset is liquid it is still possible to recover the money spent in its acquisition (or very nearly it) to start over along an alternative path. One can imagine risk premia for specific risks but there is still one general property that should protect asset holders against risks in general (including the ones not identified at the initial moment): liquidity. So liquidity premia are not simply risk premia, like all the others. Its importance derives directly from the notion of uncertainty that Keynes used in the GT, but which he came to make explicit only in his 1937 response to critics.

If this is true, the determination of asset prices offered in Chapter 17, through the concept of own rates of interest, reflects the hierarchy between allowances for the possibility of frustration of expectations, distinguishing the impact of specific risks, dealt with the method of certainty-equivalents, despite the conceptual difficulties involved in such a concept, and the attribute of liquidity, which is shared by all assets but in very different proportions. The hierarchy allows Keynes to distinguish between situations where specific risks change (for instance, credit risks when policy interest rates are raised) and that of a general rise in uncertainties, as in the case of major crises. This distinction also allows one to see in a general retreat to liquidity (a flight to liquidity), a rise in liquidity preference even if less liquid classes of assets are being dumped into markets for specific reasons (credit risks in the case of some asset-backed securities, for example). The central message is that liquidity is a protection against any and everything. When risks rise or confidence on risk calculation methods falls, liquidity premia tend to rise.

5 Conclusion

It is obvious from reading *The General Theory* that liquidity risks (and liquidity premia) are given pride of place among all classes of risk. In fact, most of the specific risks that plague the purchase of assets are either neglected by Keynes or mentioned quickly without further developments as if the author's intention was to acknowledge the relation between risk and return but to dispose of it as of secondary interest as rapidly as possible.

Two possible (actually non-exclusive) explanations are offered in this chapter for the special attention given to liquidity risks and premia in the determination of asset prices. The first was the attempt to single out what made money an asset, a form of wealth along other assets, by stressing the importance of liquidity in a world plagued by uncertainty. The second was to emphasize the proposition that while risk premia are calculated to protect the asset buyer against specified risks, liquidity premia reflect the value given by asset holders to the property of *saleability* attached, in different degrees, to each asset or class of assets. Liquid assets protect their holders against risks in general, including the ones not recognized at the moment of purchase (and therefore not covered by specific risk premia). Liquidity gives asset holders a way out of problems, be they predictable or not. Thus, Keynes's differential treatment of illiquidity risks and premia was less an expository tool but rather a reflection of how uncertainty affects attitudes of asset buyers.

Interpretations of Keynesian views and of The General Theory that follow the "liquidity preference approach," as it is the case of this book, tend to stress the second interpretation and the special role of liquidity in Keynes's theory of a monetary economy.

Notes

1 In Chapter 2 above we argued that the chapters specifically dedicated to liquidity preference in the GT may offer a misleading picture of what it means. Now we are referring to the whole book, including Chapter 17, dedicated to the analysis of asset price formation.

2 Alternatively, one can identify the liquidity premium as the reduction in the relevant rate of discount used to calculate present values that the holder is willing to accept corresponding to the value attributed to the expected power of disposal over the asset.

3 Keynes in fact presented two measures: own rates of interest and own rates of own-interest, the difference between them that the former is measured in terms of the asset itself and the second assumes relative price effects since it refers to the return on a given asset measured in any asset that may have been chosen as standard of measurement. We will follow the tradition of calling "own rates of interest" the return of a given asset measured in terms of money.

4 In the notation usually utilized by Keynes, capital letters denote money values, while small case means ratios and quotients. Thus, "q" is the ratio between Q (the value of quasi-rents) and CP (the current price of the asset being considered).

5 This is precisely the meaning Keynes proposed in the 1937 paper examined in Chapter 2, above.

6 Again, since money under normal conditions of operation of entrepreneurial economies is the most liquid of assets, it becomes the asset most capable of "lulling the disquietudes" of wealth holders.

7 Keynes explored the concept more deeply in his *A Treatise on Money* (CW 5 and 6). Afterwards the importance of secondary market characteristics in the determination of liquidity attributes was developed by Kaldor (1980) and Davidson (1978).

8 The most explicit discussion of these conditions by Keynes was made with respect to money. Keynes postulated that money in entrepreneurial economies was characterized by a few properties that kept it in short supply. The implications of such a view are explored in Chapter 4, below.

9 In fact, this statement may not be always exactly true. There is a secondary market for some securities when they reach a sufficiently low price that may warrant a bet on its recovery or some other mechanism of loss reduction. Dealing with such securities is usually the role of so-called *vulture funds*, institutional investors that specialize in buying seemingly worthless debt in the hope they can squeeze out some return out of it.

10 Obviously, if access to money is the criterion to measure liquidity, money is, by definition, the most liquid of all assets.

11 For example, loss of markets, competitors's innovations, labor problems, contractionary fiscal and monetary policies.

12 See, for example, passages where the relationship is mentioned very casually: "For the above relates primarily to the pure rate of interest apart from any allowance for risk and the like, and not to the gross yield of assets including the return in respect of risk" (CW 7: 221, see also p. 309).

Part II
Banks and money supply

4 Keynes and the endogeneity of money

1 Introduction

The critique of the quantity theory of money (QTM) was an essential step in Keynes's "long struggle to escape" the traps set by classical economics. There was no doubt, in Keynes's mind, that QTM was a theory of money demand. Trained as a Marshallian economist, Keynes understood QTM as proposing that divergences between money supply and money demand were to be resolved by movements in money demand induced by changes in money income, assuming a broadly stable money velocity.

Keynes's alternative to QTM was liquidity preference theory, which proposed that money was much more than a convenient way to transport purchasing power between the date when income was received and the date it was to be spent. Clearly, QTM as a theory of *money demand* had to be replaced by another theory of money demand, and Keynes believed to have provided one with his liquidity preference theory.

More recently, however, a group of Keynesian economists, led by Nicholas Kaldor, proposed that QTM was to be criticized *not* as a theory of money demand, as Keynes envisaged, but because of what it assumed to be the behavior of the *money supply*. This point has attracted much attention in some circles after it was raised by Kaldor. As a result of the ensuing discussions, many strands of Keynesian macroeconomics came to agree now that the money supply is endogenous in some sense. More particularly, practically all post Keynesian varieties of macroeconomic theory explicitly reject the so-called "verticalist" assumption that central banks can fully determine the money supply.[1]

Agreement, however, often stops at that. The best-known variety of endogenous money assumption in post Keynesian economics is the one identified as the "horizontalist" view, according to which the money supply curve is horizontal in the money quantity/interest rate space because suppliers of money always *fully* accommodate the demand for money at a given rate. It is, of course, intended to be a stylization of how money creation really works, but many post Keynesians take it as an actual description, close enough to the reality of modern economies, which "horizontalists" identify as *credit-money economies*.

As noted, it was Kaldor, not Keynes, who provided the inspiration for the emergence of the horizontalist hypothesis. In fact, Kaldor presented the hypothesis *against* Keynes's views on the matter, arguing that Keynes was never able to escape his "classical" training in this field. Kaldor argued that the whole liquidity preference theory was, at best, a "red-herring," giving an undue relevance to the concept of money supply.

It is well known that Keynes, in the GT, explicitly assumed that the money supply was fully controlled by the central bank. It can therefore be reasonably argued that Keynes's view in the GT can best be characterized as verticalist, not far from Milton Friedman's. Keynesians, however, often seek solace in Keynes's previous book, *A Treatise on Money*, to defend the thesis that the GT approach did not properly convey Keynes's actual views on this point. In the *Treatise*, one can find much richer and more concrete conceptions of how money is created through the interaction of banks and central banks in different monetary regimes.

The *Treatise*'s approach, however, is as distant from a horizontalist view as the GT's. In fact, the *Treatise* does embrace an endogeneity-of-money perspective, relying however on very different reasons and with very diverse implications compared to those present in the horizontalist literature. It is reasonable to assume that Keynes did not abandon the *Treatise*'s arguments on this matter when writing the GT. In fact, he stressed, in the preface to the GT, the continuity between the two books. In his words:

> The relation between this book and my Treatise on Money, which I published five years ago, is probably clearer to myself than it will be for others; ... my lack of emancipation from preconceived ideas showed itself in what now seems to me to be the outstanding fault of the theoretical parts of that work ..., that I failed to deal thoroughly with the effects of changes in the level of output.... This book, on the other hand, has evolved into what is primarily a study of the forces which determine changes in the scale of output and employment as a whole; and, whilst it is found that money enters into the economic scheme in an essential and peculiar manner, *technical monetary detail falls onto the background*.
>
> (CW 7: xv–xvii, my emphasis)

The whole analysis of monetary regimes and the role of banks and central banks in the creation of money were apparently among the "technical monetary detail" that did not find room in the GT.

In this chapter we explore the question of whether the consideration of banks and central banks offered in the *Treatise* would change the "exogenist" approach to money characteristic of the GT. We are also interested in the "debate" between Keynes and Kaldor on the means and limits of monetary policy as an instrument of aggregate demand management. We are *not*, however, directly interested in the more recent debates between horizontalists and verticalists, or between accommodationists and structuralists. We believe, of course, that the contrast between Keynes's and Kaldor's views is essential to understand the latter debates, but to develop the actual links between them would certainly demand a book in itself. The choice of Kaldor's positions to confront Keynes's is only natural, given his weight as an inspiration for the most important among horizontalist authors, at least in the English language literature. So we confine our examination to Keynes and Kaldor in the hope that this can help to illuminate the workings of monetary policy. We begin by reconstructing the way in which the money supply appears in the GT, and go backwards in time to see how the importation of the *Treatise*'s ideas about banks and central banks would fit into the GT approach, in Section 2. Section 3 is dedicated to the severe criticisms raised by Kaldor against Keynes, from which sprang the horizontalist school. A key issue opposing Keynes to Kaldor is the concept and role of liquidity, so Section 4 confronts both authors on this theme. Section 5 concludes the chapter.

2 From *The General Theory* to *A Treatise on Money*

The continuity Keynes alleged to link the *Treatise* to the GT may not be obvious to readers, at least with respect to the determination of the money supply. Banks are absent from the core model of the GT, where Keynes argues entirely in terms of central banks' decisions. Given the enormous importance the behavior of banks had always assumed in his writings prior to the GT, one is surprised to realize that all changes in money supply are explained directly by reference to the central bank. In fact, not even the central bank's behavior is actually analyzed. The central bank's choice of a given quantity of money to supply seems to be left entirely to its own discretion. One can easily understand why so many among Keynes's readers look to the *Treatise* hoping to find a more flexible treatment of the issue there.

As we will see below, the way Keynes approaches de behavior of central banks in the GT may well be a simplification but it is not essentially different from the way he described it, in much more detail, in the *Treatise*. Before moving on, it may be useful to remind readers of two points, both being crucial elements of the discussion that follows. First, the relation already explored in detail in Chapter 2 between money demand and uncertainty proposed by Keynes. Second, the role of commercial banks in the creation and allocation of money throughout the economy.

Keynes argued that holding money constituted a powerful hedge against future adverse events that are impossible to predict properly. When one cannot even imagine what kind of adversity may hit in the future, it becomes impossible to devise efficient specific hedge strategies.

Money is an efficient hedge in such situations because it is the most liquid of assets. As the unit of account for contracts, the value of money as a debt settlement vehicle is fixed.[2] As legal tender, it is convertible into any other good, service or asset, on demand.[3]

But an asset being liquid means that the holder of that particular class of assets *expects* to be able to dispose them quickly, without significant capital loss, if it is so desired. This means that holding this type of asset should allow the holder to redo her investment strategy without too much loss of time and capital value at any time. When this power of disposal is reckoned, the asset is supposed to pay "gross returns" that include a *non-monetary* yield in the form of insurance against unexpected adverse future events, along with monetary returns (such as interest, dividends, capital gains, etc.).

Liquidity in the sense just described depends of course not only on the access to secondary markets for the relevant types of assets but also on an additional requirement: that the asset in question be relatively *scarce* – that is, that future demand for the item can reasonably be *expected* to be equal or higher than future supply – so that if and when the asset holder decides to sell it she may expect that it will not cause a significant loss of value of the asset; that is, that the offer to sell will not create a significant downward pressure on its market price. To guarantee that in an entrepreneurial economy money should not lose its liquidity attribute, Keynes famously postulated three "peculiarities which commonly characterize money as we know it" (CW 7: 229–230). The peculiarities are that money elasticities of production and substitution should be very small and that, although the *real* supply of money could still change, within a given interval, because of variations in money prices of goods and services, money would still maintain its liquidity attribute in the eyes of the public, given its null or negligible carrying cost.

The term "peculiarities" to classify these properties might suggest that they constitute only a minor qualification to Keynes's argument. However, a few pages later, Keynes clarified the importance of the specification of low values for those two elasticities:

> The attribute of "liquidity" is by no means independent of the presence of these two characteristics [the negligible elasticities of production and substitution]. For it is unlikely that an asset, of which the supply can be easily increased or the desire for which can be easily diverted by a change in relative price, will possess the attribute of "liquidity" in the mind of owners of wealth. *Money itself rapidly loses the attribute of "liquidity" if its future supply is expected to undergo sharp changes.*
>
> (CW 7: 241fn, my emphasis)[4]

Keynes proposed the existence of a non-linear relation between the quantity of money and its liquidity attribute. Up to a certain level, an increase in the quantity of money should not threaten money's liquidity due to a complex pattern of feedback effects: as long as the public believes in the future stability of money's purchasing power, forward contracts, including wage contracts, will continue to be denominated and settled in money; for this reason, the expectation of price stability that sustains the liquidity of money will not be disappointed. Since the carrying cost of money is negligible,

> [t]he readiness of the public to increase their stock of money in response to a comparatively small stimulus is due to the advantages of liquidity (real or

supposed) having no offset to contend with in the shape of carrying costs mounting steeply with the lapse of time.

(Ibid.: 233)

In other words, as long as the public believes in the future stability of prices, the contract system will help to strengthen this belief and the liquidity premium of holding money will remain much higher than its carrying cost, so that the public will hold additional amounts of money in their portfolios. If trust in the future stability of prices is lost, however, the system of contracts will break down, and money will lose its liquidity attribute, as happens under hyperinflations. Money's null or negligible elasticities of production and substitution are meant to prevent this scenario from becoming true.[5]

These statements are very clear in establishing that while the money supply curve may have been proposed in the GT to be vertical just as a simplification of "technical monetary details", in no way it could be assumed to be "horizontal" without violating a property of money that turns out to be essential, in so far as the liquidity attribute of money, and its implications for Keynes's theory of effective demand, depends on its observance. In other words, if one can find in Keynes's writings an alternative to the assumption that the central bank fully controls the supply of money, it will certainly *not* be the idea that money supply is fully determined by money demand. That money has to be kept rare is an essential theoretical point, not merely a simplifying assumption, in Keynes's argument.

For the second point, one has effectively to move beyond the GT, both backwards and forwards in time. The operation of modern monetary systems was a lifelong interest of Keynes's. Two subjects in particular attracted his attention: monetary regimes and banking. Keynes's most sophisticated reflections of both subjects are presented in some chapters of the first volume of the *Treatise* (CW 5, Chapters 1 to 3), and in most of the second volume (CW 6, books 5 and 7).[6]

In the *Treatise*, the process of money creation is examined within the rules that are set by the *monetary regime* a country elects to adopt. In essence, a monetary regime defines what is money[7], how, by whom, under what circumstances and conditions it may be created, and what should serve as a standard of value.

The class of monetary regimes Keynes considered most closely was that of *managed money* regimes. In such regimes, money is managed in order to maintain its value in terms of some defined standard, which could be a commodity (as in gold exchange standards), a labor unit, or a basket of commodities. Money creation in those regimes is the result of the interaction between the central bank, which creates the monetary base, and the banking system, which creates the demand deposits that constitute the largest component of the stock of means of payment of a modern economy.

On the role and power of the central bank, Keynes in the *Treatise* is no different from Keynes of the GT. In the GT, Keynes seemed to have taken the power of the central bank to control the quantity of money as somewhat self-evident. For instance, in chapter 18 of the GT, when summarizing the "model" he proposed in the preceding chapters, he included among the givens "the quantity of money as determined by the action of the central bank" (CW 7: 247)

In the *Treatise*, Keynes stated that:

> The first necessity of a central bank, charged with responsibility for the management of the monetary system as a whole, is to make sure that it has *an unchallengeable control over the total volume of bank money created by its member banks*.
>
> (CW 6: 201, my emphasis)

Some critics could perhaps rush to the conclusion that since Keynes was writing the *Treatise* when Great Britain was still under the gold standard, he was pointing to conditions pertaining to commodity money regimes. This conclusion would be wrong, however. Keynes considered the gold-exchange standard[8] a managed money regime, where preserving the value of gold in terms of the domestic currency still gave some wide latitude to the central bank to manage the quantity of money. In particular, Keynes rejected the idea that the relevant opposition was defined between commodity money and "credit money," as became almost standard usage after Kaldor proposed it. Banks and the creation of deposits as a by-product of credit creation were fully incorporated in the *Treatise* model.[9] Moreover, as will be pointed out below, Keynes's assessment of central bank power relied on his view as to how the central bank actually created money, through its asset purchase operations, independently of the specific monetary regime under which it was operating.

A related argument that became very important in the horizontalist literature was recognized but minimized by Keynes. As will be seen in the next section, Kaldor gave much importance to the fact that central banks do not set the quantity of money or of bank reserves directly as a target. Rather, they operate by setting interest rate targets. The point is considered by Kaldor essential to sustain the thesis that since central banks usually set the level of a particular interest rate, *therefore* they have no alternative but to freely supply all reserves banks may demand at that rate.

When Keynes affirmed, however, that central banks can control the quantity of money (or, more precisely, the quantity of reserves supplied to banks), he explained that *central banks control it precisely through the choice of a value for the bank rate, that is, the cost of reserves*. In other words, Keynes was aware of the fact that central banks set an interest rate rather than imposing a direct quantitative limit on reserves. What was obviously more important to him was that the use of interest rate targets did not imply a reduction of central banks' power to control reserves (and, ultimately, bank money). On the one hand, the central bank can always set higher or lower bank rates according to whether it desires to decrease or to increase the volume of reserves supplied to banks.[10] Moreover, and even more importantly, even if the central bank was forced, for some reason, to stick to a given bank rate and to fully supply reserves at those rates according to banks' demands, it could still compensate its actions through its overall asset purchase policy. As Keynes explained:

> Thus broadly speaking, the central bank will be able to control the volume of cash and of bank money in circulation, if it can control the volume of its total assets.... Thus, the power of a central bank to manage a representative money in such a way as to conform to an objective standard, primarily depends on its ability to determine by means of a deliberate policy the aggregate amount of its own assets.
>
> (CW 6: 201)[11]

In contrast to what Kaldor would argue later, a central bank is not bound to buy only those assets that banks present to sell, even if there are in effect some groups of assets that, by costume or legal obligation, the central bank cannot refuse:

> What are those assets? A triple classification of a central bank's variable assets (i.e. assets other than bank premises, etc.) will be convenient, namely: (1) gold, (2) investments, and (3) advances. By "gold" I mean anything which the central bank cannot create itself, but from or (and) into which it is bound by law to convert its legal-tender money. By "investments" I mean any asset, other than gold, which the central bank purchases on its own initiative; that it may include bills purchased in the open market. By "advances" I mean any asset, other than gold, which the central bank has purchased in virtue of an obligation, of law or custom, to purchase which the central bank is bound or is accustomed to make such advances.
>
> (CW 6: 202)

In other words, what Keynes is proposing is that, even if the central bank is bound to make one type or another of accommodating asset purchase, it can still compensate its impact through "investment" operations, with the opposite sign and effect. There is no evidence that Keynes ever abandoned his belief that central banks were *not* powerless prisoners of banks' demands.

But the *Treatise* does not just develop in more detail similar views to those Keynes espoused in the GT. In the *Treatise* we find something else, that was left entirely out of the GT, which is a detailed analysis of how banks operate and make their balance sheet decisions and *how they create money in the process*.

Banks, in fact, had long been among Keynes's major interests. Most of the approaches to the process of money creation, then as now, considered banks to be a sort of rather passive transmission line between the central bank and the general public who demand deposits and loans. Keynes, in contrast, considered the behavior of banks the key to understand not only how money was created but how monetary variables actually affected activities in the "real" side of the economy.

In the *Treatise*, banks are explicitly characterized as decision-making entities that, like other private firms, try to maximize returns to their activities while exposing themselves to a minimum of risks. As such, they don't react mechanically either to changes in their reserves initiated by the central bank or to changes in the demand for loans coming from firms or private consumers. Their actions depend on how they balance their simultaneous desires for profitability and liquidity.

Under *normal* conditions, banks would use up all of their free reserves buying earning assets. Keeping idle reserves would not appeal to banks since there are available some classes of highly liquid assets that would still offer some interest revenue, in contrast with cash reserves that yield nothing. According to Keynes, banks had to deal with the return/liquidity dilemma the same way as other private agents – that is, by combining assets with different attributes in terms of cash returns and liquidity premia.[12]

In a way similar to his discussion of central banks' decision, Keynes proposed that:

> what bankers are ordinarily deciding is, not *how much* they will lend in the aggregate – this is mainly settled for them by the state of their reserves – but in *what forms* they will lend – in what proportions they will divide their resources between the different kinds of investment which are open to them. Broadly, there three categories to choose from – (i) bills of exchange and call loans to the money market, (ii) investments, (iii) advances to customers. As a rule, advances to customers are more profitable than investments, and investments are more profitable than bills and call loans; but this order is not invariable. On the other hand, bills and call loans are more "liquid" than investments, i.e. more certainly realizable at short notice without loss, and investments are more "liquid" than advances. Accordingly, banks are faced with a never-ceasing problem of weighing one thing against another ...
>
> (CW 6: 59)

Banks, in fact, according to Keynes, do not just discriminate between the types of assets they buy by charging different rates of interest, they may actually ration credit:

> So far, however, as bank loans are concerned, lending does not – in Great Britain at least – take place according to the principles of a perfect market. There is apt to be an unsatisfied fringe of borrowers, the size of which can be expanded or contracted, so that banks can influence the volume of investment by expanding or contracting the volume of their loans, without there being necessarily any change in the level of bank rate, in the demand schedule of borrowers, or in the volume of lending otherwise than through the banks. This phenomenon is capable, when it exists, of having great practical importance.
>
> (CW 5: 190)

When banks buy assets (including non-financial firms' debts) they create deposits and therefore increase the supply of money.[13] However, in the *Treatise*, Keynes argued that even more important than the amount of money that is thus created may be *where it is directed to*. Keynes considered the traditional approach to money circulation being treated as a unified process to be mistaken. In his view, one should distinguish between *two* money circuits in the economy, which he called *industrial circulation* and *financial circulation*. Industrial circulation referred to money (deposits) used to move goods and services around, while financial circulation moved financial assets around.[14] The quantity theory of money (QTM) recognized only the first circuit, ignoring financial circulation.[15] As a result, quantity theorists failed to understand the connection between money and financial markets and the fact, central to Keynes's approach, that in financial circulation money is not only a means of moving assets around but it is also an end in itself, an asset to be held in individual portfolios. According to Keynes, to a large extent quantity theorists' expectation that the velocity of money was stable was often falsified precisely because aggregate velocities are nothing but the average between two velocities, each of them pertaining to each of the two circulations.[16]

Even though Keynes conceded that money is fungible and may migrate from one circulation to the other, he considered that the two circuits were somewhat self-contained in the sense that the fraction of the total money stock that was dedicated to making payments in assets markets tended to remain in those markets, the same happening to the remaining fraction of the money stock in industrial circulation. If some migration took place, inflationary or deflationary pressures would ensue, depending on whether money was leaving financial for industrial circulation or the opposite.[17] *It was not the quantity of money* per se *that mattered but what kinds of transactions it was supporting.*

In this picture, banks would generate inflationary pressures when they increased advances to customers, for instance, and deflationary pressures when they bought bills and call loans or investments. How banks would determine the share of assets of each class of assets in their balance sheet depended on their profit expectations and their liquidity preferences.

Under more exceptional conditions, when uncertainty rose to extraordinary heights, banks could even prefer to accumulate non-earning reserves, if they considered that even call loans and other very short-term private assets could represent more risk than they were willing to accept. Such a situation actually happened, according to Keynes, at the outset of World War I. There is evidence that it was repeated in the 1930s.[18]

In sum, if one takes into consideration Keynes's other works besides the GT, one can actually find a theory of money endogeneity. However, this theory exhibited three specific characteristics:

1   it has very little to do with central banks, being focused on banks' liquidity preferences;
2   it does not imply that interest rates are either more or less controllable than the quantity of money; and

3   the impact of bank money creation on the economy has seldom to do with total quantities but, rather, with the specific monetary circulation to which newly-created deposits are directed.

The argument developed so far suggests that a positive-sloping, neither vertical nor horizontal, money supply curve should best describe the behavior of money supply conceived by Keynes and compatible with his theory of effective demand. Higher interest rates on loans to businesses and consumers, for instance, would induce banks to demand less liquid assets, which meant switching finance from financial to industrial circulation. In this approach, total money supply might or might not change, but its different allocation between the two circulations should have a large impact on output and employment.[19]

3 Kaldor's critique of Keynes and the creation of horizontalism

Keynes's monetary theory was subjected to heavy "friendly fire" coming from Kaldor. The criticism was not directed at specific points of the theory so much as at Keynes's monetary theory itself. Kaldor argued that *money* was not in fact a relevant concept since it was virtually impossible to set boundaries separating objects endowed with "moneyness" from those without that attribute, much less identifying any stable relationship between the quantity of money, however defined, and spending categories (Kaldor 1973a: 209).[20] Keynes's attachment to the concept of money was a legacy of his "classical" training, which he failed to let go. According to Kaldor, this was the case not only with the GT but also with the *Treatise*:

> Keynes himself never really questioned the assumption that the supply of money, however defined, is exogenously determined by the monetary authorities. At least his equations (whether those in *Treatise on Money* published in 1930, or in *The General Theory* of 1936) are not consistent with any other interpretation.
>
> (Kaldor 1986: 73)

The functions of money could be performed by different assets in various degrees: many things are "liquid," just more or less so.

Liquidity preference, as a result, was considered by Kaldor a "red herring" because, like the QTM that was its ancestor, it relied on the assumption that one could set apart unambiguously what constitutes money.[21] Even more problematic were its policy implications, since it suggested that monetary policy could be much more likely to affect macroeconomic variables than Kaldor believed to be true.

Kaldor described the money creation process as consisting of two relatively simple steps. It begins with non-financial entities, mostly firms, demanding credit from the banking system. It is assumed that credit is demanded so that those entities can purchase goods and services, such as labor services and material inputs. Kaldor assumed that these demands are accommodated by banks, allowing for the consideration of the risks involved in each individual credit request. How this process of risk evaluation and selection takes place, and its eventual impact on the supply of credit, was not made explicit by Kaldor, who seemed to believe that it does not essentially change the nature of the credit creation process he postulated. It can be inferred, however, that Kaldor considered risks pertaining to the project to be financed, or to the borrower's profile, not to the risk to banks' balance sheets, as Keynes emphasized. Be that as it may, Kaldor assumed that when the bank agrees to lend money, it creates the corresponding deposits. If the bank was loaned up, the creation of new deposits will force it to make up for its insufficiency of reserves. Again, following Kaldor's reasoning, the bank does not consider calling back previous loans or curtailing other credit operations; instead, it turns to the central bank and demands additional reserves.

Kaldor's theory of banking can be questioned from many angles, but, clearly, banks were *not* his main concern, anyway. He dedicated much more attention to the choices open to central banks in this process. In fact, he postulated that they have none but to accommodate the demand for reserves placed by banks. The central bank is supposed, initially, to set the price of these reserves, setting the interest rate to be charged from banks, but it cannot deny supplying the reserves demanded by banks at those rates. Since the demand for loans from non-financial entities is supposed to be fully accommodated by banks (except for the already mentioned risk considerations) and the demand for reserves by banks is supposed to be fully accommodated by the central bank (at a given "bank rate"), the supply curve of money (that is, of newly created deposits resulting from the whole operation) could be conveniently expressed as a horizontal curve in the interest rate/money quantity space (whatever "money quantity" might mean!).

Kaldor did dedicate much more effort to exploring the reasons why the central bank could not limit the supply of bank reserves, as Keynes suggested it should. Kaldor argued that central banks have no choice when faced with legitimate demands for reserves (that is, those demands backed by acceptable collateral or within the rules set by law or custom) but to accommodate them. Central banks can set the interest rate charged for these operations but cannot refuse to satisfy the (legitimate?) demands for reserves from banks.

Kaldor, however, did not appeal to the *legal* obligation of central banks to supply reserves under pre-specified conditions. He actually made a larger point, arguing that a refusal by the central bank to validate, through reserve creation, the demands of banks *would threaten the solvency of the banking system*. It is not obvious why *any* tightening of the market for reserves could have such a wide and deep effect. Kaldor, however, exemplified what he meant, by citing the demand for cash in the days before Christmas (and before the widespread use of credit cards and other alternative forms of payment). Kaldor asked what would happen if the central bank did not accommodate the higher demand for notes and coins before Christmas: "Of course, most people would say that it would be quite impossible to prevent the rise in the note circulation without disastrous consequences: widespread bank failures, or a general closure of the banks as a precautionary measure" (Kaldor 1973b: 266).

Still, it would not "stop Christmas buying", because new forms of payment would be created (ibid.: 267). It is difficult not to conclude that the example, proposed in all seriousness, it seems, during a direct exchange with Milton Friedman, suggests that the point was blown out of proportion and should perhaps be reevaluated.

On the other hand, Kaldor does not address Keynes's point that even if accommodation could not be refused by the central bank, the latter would still have the possibility of effecting compensatory transactions with other assets in its balance sheet. In a similar treatment to that given to banks, Kaldor seemed to consider a central bank whose range of operation is limited to "rediscounting" bank loans.

Finally, Kaldor also seemed to ignore the possibility of setting the bank rate according to a central bank's target for bank reserves, as again Keynes suggested.[22] The status of the bank rate in Kaldor's approach is unclear. At first, it is argued that a central bank can set a "price" target (the bank rate), but not a "quantity" target (the amount of bank reserves). Kaldor argued that once the central bank decides the rate to be charged, it does not have any choice but to freely supply reserves at that price. It is not clear for *how long* the central bank is bound by a given announced bank rate, or why it could not "modulate" the rate in order to limit or expand access to bank reserves, not by denying legitimate operations but by discouraging them.[23]

Kaldor's point, however, is not exactly what it seems at first sight, and what many of his followers seemed to have taken it to be – that is, that monetary policy does not work by setting quantity targets, but that it does through setting the bank rate. Kaldor in fact goes beyond that, to state that the central bank is not at liberty to set the bank rate either:

> Reliance on monetary policy as an effective stabilizing device would involve large and rapid changes in the level of interest rates and, in consequence, a high degree of instability in bond prices in the capital market. But the relative stability of bond prices is a highly important feature of an effectively functioning capital market, and of the whole credit mechanism in a capitalist economy. If bond prices were liable to vast and rapid fluctuations, the speculative risks involved in long-term loans of any kind would be very much greater than they are now, and the average price which investors would demand for parting with liquidity would be considerably higher.

> (Kaldor 1973a: 217)

Moving up or down the bank rate (and even more so when one takes into consideration its repercussions on yield curves) may directly affect the prices of assets and the solvency of financial institutions, especially those which practice maturity transformation, even more powerfully than changes in bank reserves could. At the end of the day, what Kaldor was saying is that monetary policy should not be seen as an instrument of demand management policy at all.

Moreover, Kaldor seemed to want to eat the cake and save it at the same time. He actually gave, on distinct occasions, at least three reasons to explain why central banks were powerless to control the money supply, not entirely consistent with each other. The first, and most influential, was already presented, proposing that central banks do not have a choice but to accommodate banks' demand for reserves at a given bank rate. But Kaldor also contemplated the possibility of central banks doing just what he said they could not, when he argued, in his testimony to the Radcliffe Committee, that in "countries where the [monetary]authorities pursue a restrictive policy," money velocity increases so to counteract the policy and support aggregate demand (Kaldor 1973a: 210). Finally, he also proposed a third theory of money endogeneity, according to which scarcity of money proper would lead private (and perhaps some public) agents to create money substitutes:

> What, at any time, is regarded as "money" are those forms of financial claims which are commonly used as a means of clearing debts. But any shortage of commonly used types is bound to lead to the emergence of new types; indeed, this is how, historically, first bank notes and then chequing accounts emerged.
>
> (Kaldor 1973b: 267)

Both the second and the third alternatives are theoretically hard to reconcile with the notion that central banks *always* fully accommodate the demand for reserves which underlies the horizontalist view.

4 Keynes and Kaldor on the meaning and role of liquidity

It should be obvious by now that the distance between Keynes's and Kaldor's views on money endogeneity is very large. More importantly, it relies less on matters of empirical observation than on fundamental points of theory.

The most fundamental opposition between the two seems to reside in their different views of what "liquidity" means and how it fits into the operation of a modern economy. Keynes approaches the concept of liquidity in the context of a theory of asset choice. *Liquidity is the attribute that explains why money is held in portfolios.* In this framework, liquidity relates to convertibility into money and, in this way, to any other item, liquidity means "power of disposal" over an asset. Money is an object of demand because (although not exclusively) it is the most liquid of all assets in this sense. To preserve the liquidity attribute of money led Keynes to state that constraints on its availability are a necessary condition for the regular operation of an entrepreneurial economy. Money is actually demanded not only as an asset, but also as a means of transaction (for transaction, speculative and finance motives). One has to know all the sources of demand for money to understand how supply and demand determines the interest rate, as specified by liquidity preference theory.

In contrast, for Kaldor, liquidity relates to the ability of paying for market purchases. It is the ability to serve as a means of payment that defines the liquidity of a given object. *Liquidity is the attribute that explains why money is spent.* Of course, to become a means of payment in some operation, all that is necessary is that the object be agreed upon by both parties to that transaction, so that if it is liquidity that defines "money," everything can be money, as long as there exists somebody or some group willing to accept that object as a means of payment. In this sense, there is no pre-established limit of the amount of liquidity that can (or should) be created other than the one set by the underlying transactions with goods and services that originated the demand for a means of payment. A horizontal supply curve of money does not violate any of the necessary conditions for an asset to be "liquid," in the sense proposed by Kaldor.

A second theoretical contrast between Keynes and Kaldor relates to the *nature* of liquidity. Keynes proposed a *hierarchical* concept of liquidity, where assets are not only differentiated according the "size" of their liquidity attributes but also by their nature. Money, and, particularly in modern economies, state money, is not only the most liquid of assets, but in Keynes's view, their liquidity could be seen as "intrinsic" (as long as the elasticity constraints mentioned above remain in force). Minsky called this set of assets (including in it some other obligations issued by the state) *ultimate* liquidity (Minsky 1982: 9). Other assets derive their liquidity attribute from their degree of convertibility into money. They are liquid because (and only as long as) the public *believes* they can exchange them for ultimately liquid assets quickly and without significant loss.

Kaldor's concept of liquidity, by contrast, is *flat*: there is no difference of nature between liquid assets, only of degree. Some objects may be accepted as means of payment more widely than others, so that they will be more liquid than the latter. But anybody can create liquid assets; the state does not have a "privilege" in this area.

A third contrast deals with the implications of these opposing views to monetary policy matters. Keynes believed monetary policy to be a powerful influence on aggregate demand behavior. This belief was not changed with the publication of the GT. Keynes in fact maintained it until his death. Kaldor, on the other hand, as seen in Section 3, attacked monetarism, particularly the variety practiced during the Thatcher years in Great Britain, because monetary policy could *not* achieve constructive ends. Trying to influence the economy through monetary means would disrupt its operation, as Kaldor accused prime minister Thatcher to have done. Fiscal, not monetary, policy should be recognized as the efficient instrument to manage aggregate demand.

A fourth contrast between Keynes and Kaldor referred to the role of banks. Kaldor did not put much effort in discussing the behavior of banks and its impact on the economy. Keynes, by contrast, dedicated a lifelong attention to the operation of banks and banking systems, arguably much more time than he dedicated to the study of the operation of central banks. While Kaldor exposed his brand of money endogeneity theory with reference to choices of monetary authorities, Keynes attacked the problem through the examination of bank strategies.

Finally, money endogeneity for Keynes seems better addressed as a *technical* specification of the model, between variables that are those that are not determined by the model itself, rather than being taken as givens. Kaldor, on the other hand, is motivated by his critique of monetarist attempts to rein over aggregate demand through the control of money stock. It is *controllability* that matters to Kaldor.

5 Conclusion

The use of interest rates as the main instrument of monetary policy has been presented by Kaldorians as a central piece of evidence in favor of the horizontalist hypothesis. Keynes, however, while accepting that monetary authorities do implement monetary policy through setting one or more interest rates, did not attach any importance to it beyond its identification as a modern operational procedure at the disposal of central banks. For Keynes, the question was not whether to control interest *or* reserves, but that of controlling reserves *through* interest rates.

The main points of contention between Keynes and Kaldor thus should be sought elsewhere. It is the hypothesis raised in this chapter that the contrasts between the two views of money endogeneity spring essentially from their radically different views as to what *liquidity* means: its nature and role in modern entrepreneurial economies. Keynes advanced a concept of liquidity as the power of disposal over an asset, making liquid assets, and money in particular, instruments of flexible strategies of wealth accumulation, a plus in the face of the irreducible uncertainty that surrounds the future. Some assets are considered intrinsically liquid, while others are liquid because ways were created to facilitate their marketability – that is, their convertibility into intrinsically liquid assets. Money availability is endogenously determined because it results from private decisions of wealth accumulation, oriented by the choice between expected cash returns and liquidity premia. Equally important, since money is created as a by-product of the purchase of earning assets by the banking system, for Keynes the identification of the assets banks purchase was fundamental to determining the destination of newly-created deposits, whether to industrial circulation or to financial circulation.

Keynes, when writing the *Treatise* and defining the concepts of the monetary regime that he never abandoned, did not believe that the essential distinction in monetary theory was that between commodity money and credit money, as suggested by Kaldor, but that between representative money regimes, particularly between fiat money and managed money. Bank deposits are the main type of means of payment in both types of regime.

As already noted, at the end of the day, the proof of the pudding is the eating. The financial crisis initiated in 2007–2008 in the United States, later spread to many other areas, offers a particularly apt test event for theories that emphasize the importance of liquidity. In chapter 9, which closes this book, we will try to argue that Keynes's approach survived very well the test of adherence to facts.

Notes

1 Verticalism is believed to be a trading mark of monetarism, although it is also shared by many other theoretical traditions, including the neoclassical synthesis.

2

> The fact that contracts are fixed, and wages are usually somewhat stable, in terms of money unquestionably plays a large part in attracting to money so high a liquidity-premium. The convenience of holding assets in the same standard as that in which future liabilities may fall due and in a standard in terms of which the future cost of living is expected to be relatively stable is obvious.
>
> > (CW 7: 236–237)

Stressing and exploring this point has always been one of the pillars of Paul Davidson's writings on Keynes. See, for instance, Davidson (1978), the most complete presentation of his views.

3 Keynes, in the *Treatise*, also emphasizes the importance of acceptance by the State in the payment of taxes of a given means to give it moneyness (CW 5). Under the extreme conditions of high and hyperinflations, money may (and usually does) lose this convertibility attribute (see Cardim de Carvalho 1992, Chapter 11).

4 See also, in the same direction, Dow (1997: 65).

5

> I conclude, therefore, that the commodity in terms of which wages are expected to be most sticky, cannot be one whose elasticity of production is not least, and for which the excesses of carrying costs over liquidity premium is not least.
>
> > (CW 7: 238)

6 The basic principles of Keynes's theory of banking were to become central elements of his ICU/Bancor plan to create an international monetary system after World War II (see CW 25).

7 Or, more precisely, what constitutes *state* money. Money may be a commodity, such as gold or silver, or be *representative* money, such as *fiat* money or *managed* money, as in contemporary systems.

8 In the gold exchange standard, by contrast with the "classic" gold standard, a representative of gold – paper money issued by the Bank of England – circulates instead of gold or alongside it. Of course, the need to maintain convertibility imposed limits on the ability of the Bank to issue paper money, but those limits could be made more or less elastic if necessary.

9 In the post-publication debates around the GT with Bertil Ohlin, Keynes was at pains to clarify his view that while money (in the form of bank deposits) was created mostly as a result of credit operations, it was the demand and supply of money that interested him, not the operation of the credit market *per se*. In fact, he insisted that confusing credit with money was at the root of the inability of his opponents in this matter to understand the theory of liquidity preference. Keynes's side of the debate with Ohlin is reproduced in CW 14.

10 In fact, that had always been Keynes's view. In his Tract on Monetary Reform, when Keynes was still "as orthodox on the subject of the Quantity Theory as any earlier economist, and more orthodox than many" (Kahn 1984: 53), he held, as he actually did on every occasion, that setting the interest rate was the instrument used by monetary authorities to control the amount of liquidity in the economy:

> It is desirable … that the whole of the [bank] reserves should be under the control of the authority responsible for this, which, under the above proposals, is the Bank of England. The volume of paper money, on the other hand, would be consequential, *as it is at present*, on the state of trade and employment, bank-rate policy and

the Treasury bill policy. The governors of the system would be bank-rate and Treasury bill policy, the objects of government would be stability of trade, prices, and employment, and the volume of paper money would be a consequence of the first (*just – as I repeat – as it is in the present*) and an instrument of the second, the precise arithmetical level of which could not as need not be predicted.

(CW 4: 153–154, my emphasis)

11 This point was also emphasized by Smithin (2013: 245, his emphasis): "The question, now, is whether control of the money supply must *necessarily* be exercized indirectly ... Or, can the nominal 'quantity of money,' on the contrary, be *directly* controlled by the central bank?"

12 Why would commercial banks, which have the power to create money, be concerned with the liquidity of their balances will be explored in Chapter 5, next.

13 As Keynes's Cambridge students during the Michaelmas Term of 1932 noted in their notebooks, Keynes emphasized that "Money is created when banks buy debts. Money is destroyed when banks get rid of debt, by selling it or having it discharged" (Rymes 1989: 67). A very interesting exchange on this particular point involved Keynes, Reginald McKenna and Lord Macmillan in the February 21, 1930 session of the Macmillan Committee, where McKenna made very forcefully the point that banks create deposits when they make loans, instead of depending on depositors to finance them, receiving Keynes's full support. (CW 20: 87, 90)

14

By *industry* we mean the business of maintaining the normal process of current output, distribution and exchange and paying the factors of production their incomes for the various duties which they perform from the first beginning of production to the final satisfaction of the consumer. By *finance*, on the other hand, we mean the business of holding and exchanging existing titles to wealth (other than exchanges resulting from the specialization of industry), including stock exchange and money market transactions, speculation and the process of conveying savings and profits into the hands of entrepreneurs.

(CW 5: 217)

15 This oversight actually persists even now. A number of orthodox monetary economists have been insisting that changes in the quantity of money promoted by central banks could have be having expansionary effects on asset markets, increasing prices, but which were ignored by monetary authorities.

16 Keynes developed the argument about velocities of circulation in CW 6, Chapter 24.

17 The terms "inflationary" and "deflationary" had somewhat different meanings at the time than they have today. Basically, they referred to movements either of money supply or of money income. Inflating money supply meant increasing the amount of money in circulation which should lead to, or at least be correlated with, expanding nominal income. It was only after World War II that the terms inflation and deflation were specialized to the description of the behavior of prices.

18 See, for instance, Morrison (1967). The point is further explored in Chapter 5, next.

19 Keynes's approach to banks and monetary circulation was a development of some of his oldest intuitions. It inspired authors like Davidson, Minsky, Kregel, Dow, Bibow among others, to apply liquidity preference theory to explain the behavior of banks. See Chapter 5, below.

20 Kaldor (1986: 8) praised the Radcliffe Report, in which he recognized close kinship with his own ideas, for stating that:

[t]hough we do not regard the supply of money as an unimportant quantity, we view it as only part of a wider structure of liquidity in the economy.... *It is the whole liquidity position* that is relevant to spending decisions and our interest in

the supply of money is due to its significance in the whole liquidity picture.... The decision to spend thus depends upon liquidity in the broad sense, not upon immediate access to the money.... The spending is not limited by the amount of money in existence but it is related to the amount of money people think they can get hold of, whether by receipts of income (for instance from sales), by disposal of capital assets or by borrowing.

21 "Liquidity preference" turns out to have been a bit of a red herring – not the "crucial factor" which, in the view of the great economists of Keynes's generation, such as Dennis Robertson or Jacob Viner, and, of a later generation, Harry Johnson or James Tobin, alone enabled Keynes to argue that an economy can be in equilibrium at less than full employment, It has nothing to do with that at all" (Kaldor, 1986: 26). Kaldor interprets liquidity preference theory as consisting merely of a qualification on the QTM assumption that money velocity is stable. For this reason, "once we realize that the supply of money is endogenous (it varies automatically with demand, at a given rate of interest), 'liquidity preference' and the behavior of the velocity of circulation ceases to be important" (ibid.: xvii).

22 In fact, Kaldor *did* acknowledge the point:

But the Central Bank cannot close the "discount window" without endangering the solvency of the banking system; they must maintain their function as a "lender of last resort". ... *all they can do is to raise or lower the discount rates when the growth of money stock runs ahead of, or behind, the target.*

(Kaldor 1986: 25)

However, he did not extract any conclusion from this clause.

23 As we already saw, Keynes did not ignore the fact that setting the bank rate was the operational procedure favored by central banks, but he did not make much of it, since the central bank could, in principle, move the rate up and down according to its objectives with respect to the amount of reserves in the banking system.

5 Liquidity preference of banks and crises

1 Introduction

The purpose of the chapter is to argue in favor of the extension of liquidity preference theory to explain portfolio choices of banks and its consequences. Among the latter, one counts the possibility of adding some notion of financial dynamics to the operation of entrepreneurial economies described in the GT, which is essential to the understanding of financial crises. We proceed therefore by reconstructing the concept of liquidity preference as applied to banks, before and beyond the GT, to arrive at a form of the theory useful to analyze contemporary events. Then, we address directly the reasons why banks should also have liquidity preference even when it is acknowledged that they are also creators of money, an issue about which many equivocal statements have been made by critics of liquidity preference theory. The last section concludes.

2 The meaning of liquidity preference: liquidity premium and asset prices

In the last chapter we stated that in the GT the banking sector is a ghost. We can find consumers and entrepreneurs, savers and investors, workers and firms, but banks are mentioned only in the context of references to specific empirical situations. There are debts, of course, but one does not know who issued them. In fact, the own-rates of interest model is developed as if wealth-holders were financing their asset acquisitions with unlimited resources of unspecified origin. As presented in The GT, liquidity preference is a model of *asset choice*, not of *balance sheet choice*.

The approach would be completed, however, with Hyman Minsky's (1975) extension of the own-rates of interest model to include the issuance of liabilities. Now, wealth-holders should consider not only expected returns from the purchase of assets but also the cash outflow commitments that the issuance of liabilities represented. As Minsky put it, the fundamental decision now was how to reconcile cash inflows expected to result from the purchase of assets with the cash outflows committed with the issuance of liabilities and the margins of safety to be respected in the reconciliation between the two to guarantee that debts could be paid (and bankruptcy avoided) even if asset revenue expectations were to be disappointed. In the extended model, prices of assets still depend on supply and demand, but demand is now more complex, comprising not only the attributes of the assets themselves but also of the financing channels available to their buyer.

3   Liquidity preference of banks

Keynes's first inkling of a specific behavior of banks toward liquidity seems to have been his analysis of the turbulences generated by World War I on London capital markets.[1] London was then the main financial hub of the world economy. Investors and borrowers turned to the city to do their deals and local brokers worked as intermediaries, assuming debts with banks to make short term loans to securities buyers. When the war began, payments were disrupted and brokers had to settle their debts with banks while being unable to collect their loans. To prevent the market's collapse, the Bank of England extended a line of credit to banks to induce them to roll over brokers's loans. Given the increased uncertainties created by the war as to when markets would in fact return to normality, banks did borrow from the Bank of England but refused to roll over brokers' debts or to extend them new loans. Uncertain about the probability of actually recovering their credits to brokers they preferred to hold low-earning or non-earning liquid assets to buying paying assets. As a result, credit supply contracted and fresh difficulties were created for the overall economy.

The issue seems to have re-emerged, which is not entirely surprising, only in the context of the crises of the late 1920s and early 1930s. Two works stand out in this respect. A short article, reprinted in *Essays in Persuasion*, developed the idea of safety margins adopted by banks in their function as intermediaries between lenders and borrowers, which exposed them to credit risks.[2] Banks would react to changes in the level of uncertainty by strengthening their safety margins (which led to a reduction in credit supply). Sometimes, however, banks would be surprised by an adverse shock too strong to be neutralized by their margins, and a financial collapse would ensue.

The other piece, more pertinent perhaps for the present discussion, was contained in volume two of *A Treatise on Money*, on *The Applied Theory of Money* (CW 6). In that work, as shown in Chapter 4, above, Keynes proposed a typical balance sheet to characterize banks' choices, where banks issued one liability, deposits, and bought three classes of assets: bills of exchange and call loans, investments and advances to customers. Assets differed in their liquidity premia and money returns. Call loans were more liquid and less remunerative than investments, and investments kept a similar relationship to advances to customers. Given the amount of resources they could amass in the form of deposits, the problem for banks was to structure the asset side of their balance sheets in such a way as to reach a desired overall liquidity premium and desired money return. When uncertainty increased, choices would be biased toward more liquid assets at the cost of reducing the profitability of the bank. When uncertainty is decreased, the bias was in favour of illiquid assets increasing the bank's returns. When rising uncertainty affected the banking sector as a whole, the result of rising uncertainty would be the reduction of credit (that is, a reduction in the advances to customers) in favor of an increase of call loans and investments.

It may be more than a little surprising that Keynes's first follower down this path was probably Milton Friedman. Friedman and Schwartz (1963) relied on the concept of liquidity preference of banks to explain the perseverance of the post-contraction stagnation in the United States and attributed to the failure by the Fed to understand it the adoption of tough monetary policy.[3] The evidence utilized by Friedman and Schwartz was, in fact, of the type suggested by Keynes, the evolution of prices of liquid and relatively illiquid assets, rather than merely the accumulation of reserves (Friedman and Schwartz 1963: 453). Based on the price evidence, Friedman and Schwartz (1963) concluded that reserve accumulation was not due, as conventionally accepted then and since, to the absence of willing and able borrowers, but to a conscious drive by banks to increase their liquidity in the highly uncertain environment of the American economy in the 1930s.[4]

Hyman Minsky brought the subject back to the economics of Keynes through his stress on the importance of considering balance sheet maturity mismatches to explain asset accumulation strategies and their consequences. Minsky's argument is, by now, well known: the decision to purchase assets depends on the nature of the liabilities that will be issued to finance the operation. Ultimately, asset revenues have to be enough to validate debt commitments when they come due. An asset buyer has to be solvent (which happens when the net present value of assets is at least as large as the net present value of liabilities) but she also has to be liquid (to be able to honor her debts *when* they come due). Building illiquid positions, as it happens in the case of what Minsky (1982) called speculative and Ponzi portfolios, is the essential bet that asset holders have to make in capitalist economies. In Minsky's model, asset buyers are exposed to insolvency risk when they leverage their investments, and to illiquidity risk when they accept maturity mismatches between assets and liabilities.

Banks, as they exist in modern capitalist economies, face similar dilemmas to those suffered by households and non-financial firms but, in contrast to the latter, cannot avoid being illiquid. Issuing shorter-term liabilities to buy longer-term assets is essential to banks whose reasons to exist include liquidity and maturity transformation. Financial fragility is a non-negotiable condition of modern banking systems.[5] For Minsky, the dilemmas are similar to the ones suffered by households, but the impacts on the economy are far more important:

> The essential liquidity preference in a capitalist economy is that of bankers and businessmen, and the observable phenomena that indicate the state of liquidity preference are the trends of business and banker balance sheets.
>
> (Minsky 1982: 74)

After Minsky, other authors relying on liquidity preference theory to explain the behavior of banks include Jan Kregel (1984/85), Sheila and Alexander Dow

(1989), and Cardim de Carvalho (1999). In these works, more emphasis is given to implications of the hypothesis, particularly with respect to the debate around the controllability of the money supply (which opposes "verticalists" to "horizontalists"), discussed in the preceding chapter. Taking liquidity preference of banks into consideration leads to the acknowledgement that banks may not be just the transmission belt linking the general public and monetary authorities, as it is assumed both by verticalists and horizontalists. Keynes acknowledged that banks could "sterilize" expansive policies initiated by the central bank, as he said it happened during World War I. Even under more normal conditions banks could influence the operation of the "real" economy by directing the finance they create to either the industrial or the financial circulations.

4 Why do banks have liquidity preference?

Households and firms accumulate liquid assets, including money, despite their normally low yields firstly because they recognize that their expectations as to the future returns of assets can be disappointed, but also because debts contracted to finance the purchase of those assets will have to be honored no matter whether their revenue expectations have or have not been disappointed. Since households and firms do not produce money, to raise the probability that their debts will be honored and bankruptcy will be avoided they have to accumulate, or ensure timely access to, the necessary amounts of means of payment at the points in time when payments come due. If they were allowed to pay their debts in IOUs of their own issuance, there would be no need to hold any low-earning highly liquid asset in their portfolios.

The reason for banks to exhibit liquidity preference may be less obvious. After all, the largest component of the stock of means of payment outstanding in any modern entrepreneurial economy are demand deposits at commercial banks. Bank liabilities are part of the money supply, so banks can actually pay debts with IOUs of their own issuance. Or can they?

Post Keynesians explain the *moneyness* of bank deposits through their closeness to legal tender. It is government debt which is the bedrock of liquidity in a capitalist economy. As Minsky (1982: 9) observed:

> The ultimately liquid assets of an economy consist of those assets whose nominal value is independent of the functioning of the economy. For an enterprise economy, the ultimately liquid assets consist of the domestically owned government debt outside government funds, Treasury currency, and specie.

Bank deposits became money because of the support structures that were created to guarantee their prompt convertibility at par into legal tender.[6] Moneyness is not a natural attribute. It is conferred to an asset by those support structures. The public came to accept bank deposits as a close (or even superior, given its higher convenience of use) substitute to legal tender because it trusts those support structures. The State has in fact shared its power to create money with the banking sector by extending its guarantees to the latter's demand liabilities, thereby ensuring their convertibility into currency at fixed prices. That is why banks can make payments to households and firms by issuing their own IOUs, that is, by creating deposits, when they buy earning assets from the public.

Banks cannot, in contrast, pay each other or, more importantly, the central bank with these IOUs. They need an *outside* form of money to do it. Even more important, should the public lose confidence on the State support structures for any reason and demand redemption of deposits, banks have to be prepared to honor them not with other IOUs, but with legal tender. As Keynes pointed out in the Treatise on Money, banks too have to consider the likelihood of having to make these payments when they decide the composition of their asset portfolios.

5 Liquidity preference of banks and crises

An implication of acknowledging liquidity preferences is to consider that portfolio (or balance sheet) choices are sensitive not only to variations in the relevant interest rates but also to changes in perceived uncertainties. As uncertainty rises, low-yield liquid assets become increasingly in demand in detriment of less liquid assets that are forced to raise their offered money returns if they are to attract holders. If one traces a liquidity preference schedule in the traditional interest rate/money demand space, an autonomous increase in liquidity preference of this kind is represented as a shift upwards of the whole function. Since demand for liquid assets is strengthened, demand for illiquid assets will fall below supply, reducing their prices. As some of the most illiquid assets are reproducible goods as, notably, capital goods, excess supplies will lead to reduced production and, thus, lower output and employment. Through the Keynesian multiplier, this negative impulse is amplified into a larger still loss of aggregate income. This is a central proposition of the economics of Keynes, no matter *who* is demanding assets, whether households and non-financial firms or banks themselves.[7]

A key factor, therefore, to determine the dynamics of such a situation is how far banks can count on the public accepting deposits as perfect substitutes for legal tender. The public will accept those liabilities as perfect substitutes for money to the extent they trust government institutions to timely honor the guarantees they extend to bank deposits. If depositors suspect that these guarantees may not be honored, or even not honored timely, bank runs may take place even in the presence of deposit insurance schemes, as it happened in the case of Northern Rock bank in the United Kingdom in 2007.

Of course, if the economy is prosperous, supporting institutions lose their visibility and immediacy since the expectation prevails that banks' investments will pay and allow redemption of deposits out of their own resources if needed. But in times like this, when confidence is strong, the influence of liquidity preference on behavior can only be weak. During crises or other moments of heightened uncertainty, however, ignoring variations in the demand for liquid assets motivated by an autonomous rise in liquidity preference eliminates the possibility to understand the defensive portfolio strategies that tend to dominate the operation of the financial system and to strengthen whatever contractive tendency the economy may be already exhibiting. For banks, in these moments credit and other risks tend to sharply increase, compromising at the eyes of the depositors the trustworthiness of their liabilities. Under such circumstances, one can hardly be surprised to verify a rise of banks' own liquidity preferences.

Can we take modern banks to be immune to collapses of confidence? The question is in part rhetorical since the current crisis has unequivocally shown they are not. Of course, in the case of bank deposits there are many factors sustaining their moneyness, such as the action of central banks as lenders of last resort and deposit insurers.

Most analysts would probably agree, at least until recently, that the institutions created in reaction to the bank runs of the Great Depression had all but eliminated the problem of confidence in the convertibility of deposits and, by implication, in the solidity of banks themselves. As a consequence, banks' liquidity preference should also have been largely attenuated, perhaps to the point of becoming irrelevant. Particularly for banks that are *too big to fail*, survival seemed to be taken as a given, not as a concern. Their liabilities, therefore, and not only deposits, should be considered very good substitutes for legal tender, equally able to satisfy the public's demand for liquid assets.

The financial crisis initiated in the United States in 2007 shattered these views. "Classic" bank runs, of course, remained a rare (but not unheard of) phenomenon. Amid abundant news about bank problems in 2007 and 2008, depositors didn't seem to panic, apparently trusting the ability of the authorities to safeguard deposits and other classes of bank liabilities. In contrast, confidence collapsed *within* the financial system. The sudden realization that all classes of financial institutions were much more vulnerable to adverse shocks than initially imagined led to a sudden increase in liquidity preferences that not only caused a widespread collapse of prices for less liquid assets (including some that only became less liquid in the occasion) but also led to strong credit rationing among financial entities.[8]

The dramatic shift upwards of the liquidity preference schedule of financial institutions responded to at least five sources of increased uncertainty:

1   doubts about the willingness and the ability of central banks to act as lenders of-last-resort given the recent adherence of monetary authorities in many countries to inflation-targeting regimes;
2   doubts about the eligibility of shadow banks' liabilities to access government guarantees;
3   the cost of appealing to government support being interpreted as signaling weakness;
4   disruptions in the interbank market for reserves; and
5   doubts about how safe dependence on securitized markets as sources of funding was under crisis conditions.

The first source of uncertainty related to the extent to which banks could count on the support of central banks in the case of a sudden need for large injections of liquidity. With the major exception of the Federal Reserve, the overwhelming majority of central banks in the largest or most important economies then adopted some form of inflation-targeting, acknowledging no other goal than keeping inflation under control.[9] Particularly remarkable, the European Central Bank didn't even possess the mandate or the instruments to intervene in favor of maintaining financial stability in the euro area. Moreover, the chairmen and executive boards that directed the ECB since its creation had been remarkably consistent in the defense of an extremely conservative view of the bank's mission. Could this institution be relied upon to understand how much liquidity was needed when the financial crisis broke out and to act as needed to preserve financial stability?

During most of 2011, the same doubt returned as the ECB resisted calls to provide the necessary liquidity to deal with the sovereign debt crisis in the eurozone. It was only in December 2011, after Chairman Trichet was replaced by Mario Draghi, that the Bank finally intervened to contain and, at least temporarily, revert the liquidity crisis in public debt securities in the European Union. By providing three-year funding at low interest rates to European banks and accepting public debt securities as collateral, the ECB in fact increased the liquidity of securities that had lost this attribute in the eyes of private investors. Banks can now keep them in their portfolios because they became perfect substitutes to cash itself, being assets that could be easily transformed into cash if necessary.

The second source of uncertainty was fed by the acknowledgement that even if the monetary authorities were in fact willing to intervene to try and preserve financial stability it was far from obvious how to accomplish it given that a major share of the liabilities under threat had been issued by institutions that constituted the so-called *shadow* banking system, not eligible for central bank support. The shadow banking system comprises divisions of existing institutions, such as investment banks, as well as other entities, some of which were created precisely to circumvent regulatory constraints. Special purpose vehicles, conduits, etc. all operated alongside banks and investment banks, oftentimes in close relation with them, exposing the latter to risks generated by those shadowy institutions and deals, but beyond the reach of both regulatory and supporting institutions.

The third source of uncertainty sprang from the possible consequences for a financial institution of appealing for government support. Besides the usual aversion to attracting the attention of authorities to one's institution and to practices and innovations that financial firms would have preferred perhaps to keep opaque to supervisors, it was also necessary to consider how clients, investors and the general public would take the news that government support was needed amid an already volatile environment. The stigma that is assumed to accompany every appeal for help could be catastrophic in the middle of a situation already verging on panic.

The fourth source of uncertainty was the operation of the interbank markets for reserves which became an important source of funding for banks in recent years. As the crisis showed how opaque were the data about individual banks, as banks judged until that time by the market and by regulators to be solid showed themselves to be, in reality, extremely fragile, trust among banks crashed. Banks exhibiting high regulatory capital coefficients, and praised for their risk management practices, were brought down in a few days when interbank markets dried down.

Finally, in recent decades even commercial banks had come to rely more and more on the issuance of securities instead of accepting deposits as sources of funding for their asset purchases. Commercial papers, asset-backed securities, and other types of securities had become increasingly important classes of liabilities for banks and investment banks and the collapse of those markets in the aftermath of the subprime crisis threatened to close their access to liquidity sources precisely in the moments liquidity was needed the most. These types of securities did not count on government guarantees. Banks themselves were the guarantors of securities and this did not seem enough anymore. In other words, central banks respecting the traditional boundaries of their jurisdictions would be doubly ineffective: on the one hand, they would not reach the so-called shadow banking system, because it is constituted by financial entities other than commercial banks; but even if the monetary authorities restricted their action to commercial banks, it could be unable to stabilize even the traditional banking system, since modern commercial banks funded a large share of their activities through commercial paper issuance rather than by deposit acceptance.

The strong increase in liquidity preference by banks and other financial institutions as a reaction to these uncertainties should not be surprising. It manifested itself in a sharp increase in the demand for the most liquid assets, central bank reserves and Treasury securities, with the concomitant attempts to dump illiquid assets, practically at any price. This caused the reemergence of a Fisher-type debt deflation process in which asset prices collapsed leading to contagion to other, until then healthy, financial institutions that held similar assets in their balance sheets. In the language of Keynes in the *Treatise on Money*, banks tried to dump both advances to customers and investments, to increase their holdings of fully liquid assets. The result was credit rationing to non-financial borrowers and the transformation of the financial crisis into an economic crisis.[10]

The macroeconomic impact of rising liquidity preferences of banks was to be the way through which rising uncertainties imparted deflationary tendencies on the overall economy, causing a rise in unemployment and a contraction of output. This is a process where a plethora of feedback effects reinforce the initial contractive impulse. A recession increases credit risks, accentuates existing uncertainties felt by the public with respect to the health of banks, increasing the possibility of "runs," which strengthens banks' liquidity preferences, initiating a new round of deflationary pressures.[11] Even when the feedback effects are eventually detained as a result of some exogenous intervention (or of a natural exhaustion of the process of contraction), the memory of risks and losses may be enough to keep banks' liquidity preferences high, preventing economic recovery, as Friedman and Schwartz (1963) alleged to have happened in the 1930s.

The action of monetary authorities was swift and avoided the potentially large number of bankruptcies among financial institutions that could have happened if debt-deflation had been allowed to proceed unchallenged but the ECB seems to have retreated into a very conservative reading of its "mission" at the same time in which very orthodox policy views to deal with the crisis became dominant in the European Union, under the leadership of the German government. Nevertheless, while financial institutions were preserved, the near-death experience seems to have moved their liquidity preference schedule up to a new level from which they are reluctant to come down. On the other hand, as recovery has shown itself elusive so far both in the United States and in the European Union, and new threats have emerged, central banks have suffered strong pressures to extend the reach of their intervention.

These pressures have been heeded reluctantly, particularly in Europe. The ECB has been at the receiving end of a particularly strong pressure to maintain liquidity conditions in sovereign debt securities markets for eurozone members. Dissent in its governing board seems to be strong and support policies are adopted or announced only after painful episodes of political conflict. No matter who is right in this debate, the result can only be increased uncertainty, not only in financial markets. It should not be surprising that evidence is still accumulating that despite the implementation of easing monetary policies in the United States and Western Europe, banks still cling to liquid assets in detriment of less liquid investments and advances to customers, securities markets are unable to properly recover and other, less important, financing channels for private borrowers remain clogged.

6 Conclusion

Rising liquidity preferences can explain a collapse of the demand for illiquid assets that may trigger a crisis. Moreover, it can also explain why, after a serious crisis or adverse shock, it may be so difficult for an economy to recover its normal production and employment levels or rates of growth. Keynes, in the GT, seemed to think that crises were seldom due to rising liquidity preferences or interest rates. His bet was on collapses of the marginal efficiency of capital as the likely cause of downturns in modern entrepreneurial economies (See CW 7: 317/318). A rise in liquidity preference, however, would strengthen and entrench the contractive impulse, pushing the economy farther downwards, and could also make a recovery more difficult while asset holders preferred liquid to illiquid (particularly reproducible capital) assets. A rise in the *liquidity preferences of banks* would act in the same direction, possibly making those problems even more intractable for policy makers.

Some of the original critics of the liquidity preference theory argued that the theory was unconvincing because they could not find evidence of an increase in the holdings of liquid assets. Keynes pointed out that this was not the effect he expected since a higher demand for liquid assets would not increase existing stocks of the items, it would instead raise their prices. Changes in liquidity preferences should thus explain prices of assets, not their amounts unless mechanisms of new asset creation were also made part of the theory (as some authors, notably Paul Davidson, actually worked out for reproducible assets).[12]

The extension of the theory to banks' portfolio choices does not change the principle in any essential way. Price data are still the main sort of information required to test the model validity. Of course, the price of the most liquid of assets, bank reserves, is policy-controlled and not necessarily sensitive to liquidity demands. However, particularly during the worst period of the 2007–2008 financial crisis, a good indicator of rising liquidity preferences was given by the ratio between policy-controlled and market-controlled prices of reserves, such as the LIBOR. As more and more institutions were struggling to reconstitute their liquidity reserves in private markets, prices of reserves in private markets tended to surge in comparison to policy-controlled rates.

An even more direct evidence of the shift toward liquid assets was the comparison between the yields on securities widely acknowledged as being highly liquid, such as United States Treasury securities, and less liquid assets, like private securities or even public securities issued by less trusted governments. Again, during the 2007–2008 crisis, the spread between these classes of securities reached dimensions that spoke eloquently of the flight to safety that followed in particular the bankruptcy of the Lehman Brothers investment bank. Similar, and related, effects could also be found in the movements of exchange rates that follow like a shadow changes in the demand for safe assets, like United States Treasuries, away from riskier securities.

Of particular interest is the behavior of prices of assets that were considered highly liquid before the crisis and rapidly became illiquid afterwards. Securities like CDOs suffered a rapid change in the public's appreciation simultaneously with the slowdown or downright paralysis of their secondary markets, allowing the estimation of the impact of sudden loss of perceived liquidity on their market values.

In a longer-term perspective, however, one can go beyond price data to also include quantitative data. In particular, the accumulation of voluntary reserves has increased its importance, leading some analysts to question the efficacy of policy initiatives of the quantitative easing type. Of course, proper analysis of data showing an increase in reserve accumulation has to distinguish between the speculative demand for reserves and the precautionary demand for reserves. The speculative motive refers to expectations that paying assets will have their market prices lowered even further than they have already had, so that the accumulation of reserves is just *money in waiting*, not a demand for money as such. The precautionary demand for reserves, on the other hand, is the core of the concept of liquidity preference of banks, the demand for money to hold when the future is so uncertain no commitment to particular investments is advisable. The ability to get rid of assets in the case the future turns out different from what was expected when they were bought, for whatever reason, is a plus when uncertainty increases. One of the most fundamental propositions advanced by Keynes in the GT, that is, that the demand for liquid assets by private agents in the face of rising uncertainty seems efficient for the individual but is socially perverse, applies to banks as well, or even more. In the same sense, only the intervention of an *outsider*, free from the fears that plague private agents who are vulnerable to illiquidity and insolvency, can put a stop to financial crises. The need for the intervention of governments and central banks in these situations is as strong now as it was in the 1930s.

In sum, the concept of liquidity preferences of banks seems to be alive and well, with its usefulness unequivocally demonstrated by the events that have characterized not only the financial crisis of 2007–2008 but also its aftermath, that as a matter of fact is still unfolding. Conventional monetary theories converged with some non-orthodox approaches, such as Kaldor's, to minimize the role of banks, and of their liquidity preference, in the dynamics of modern capitalist economies, contrary to what Keynes proposed in 1930 in his *Treatise on Money*. Too much stress, perhaps, was given to the role (and power) of central banks, and too little attention was given, in macroeconomic theories, to banks and financial institutions and markets (with a few exceptions that have been recognized of late). Important crises have left deep imprints in economic thought. It is very likely that a new look at the relevance of a theory of banks' liquidity preference will be one of them in the near future.

Notes

1 The oldest discussion I am aware of was published in *The Economic Journal* in September 1914. It is reproduced in CW 11: 238/271.
2 The article is "The consequences to the banks of the collapse of money values," included in CW 9. This article was to become one of Minsky's central references when building his own theory of financial fragility and instability.
3

> No doubt changes in the demand for loans and in the supply of investments, and the large increase in available reserves produced by the gold inflows – all of which constituted changes in the supply of assets for banks to hold – played a role in the shifts in asset composition. *However, the major factor was not those but rather a shift in the liquidity preference of commercial banks, that is, a change in the demand by banks for assets, which is to say, in the portfolio composition they sought to attain for any given structure of yields.*
>
> (Friedman and Schwartz 1963: 453, emphasis added)

4

> The shift in liquidity preferences of banks was destined to be temporary. To judge by the experience of earlier episodes, the passage of time without any extensive series of bank failures would have dulled the fears of bank managers, leading them to set a lower premium on liquidity. In any case, the establishment of FDIC, which was accompanied by a dramatic reduction in the rate of bank failures, provided additional assurance against the occurrence of "runs" of the kind that produced the shift in liquidity preferences. Such assurance, while by no means clear at the start of the FDIC, eventually became increasingly clear, but still it took time

for banks to adapt their behavior to that new fact. It is therefore not surprising that the ratio of cash assets to total assets continued rising until 1940.

(Friedman and Schwartz 1963: 458–459)

A student of Milton Friedman's, George Morrison, wrote a PhD dissertation on the same subject, adding some evidence. See Morrison (1967).

5 One should consult Kregel (1998) for a theoretical and historical account of the evolution of modern banking in some advanced economies.

6 Legal tender is the object the law of contracts mandates creditors to accept in liquidation of a debt. See Davidson (1978).

7 As Keynes (1937: 665, 666) observed:

In order that the entrepreneur may feel himself sufficiently liquid to embark on the transaction, someone else has to agree to become, for the time being at least, more illiquid than before.... In a simplified schematism, designed to elucidate the essence of what is happening, but one which, in fact, is substantially representative of real life, one would assume that "finance" is wholly supplied during the interregnum by the banks; and this is the explanation of why their policy is so important in determining the pace at which new investment can proceed. Dr Herbert Bab has suggested to me that one could regard the rate of interest as being determined by the interplay of the terms on which the public desires to become more or less liquid and those on which the banking system is ready to become more or less unliquid. This is, I think, an illuminating way of expressing the liquidity-theory of the rate of interest; but particularly so within the field of "finance."

8 Alan Greenspan (2010) judged the 2007–2008 financial crisis to have been worse than that of the early 1930s precisely because the former completely disrupted short term interfinancial lending, something he argued did not happen in the Depression.

9 But the commitment of US authorities to safeguard financial stability by their insistence on the importance of curbing moral hazard culminated in the disastrous decision taken September 2008 to shut down the investment bank Lehman Brothers.

10 See Chapter 9 for a longer, more detailed argument.

11 A "run" can happen in modern conditions in different ways when compared to the 1930s. Depositors might feel protected by deposit insurance, but *repo* creditors or ABS holders, for instance, know they cannot count on official support. A run nowadays may consist, thus, in the simple refusal to renew a repo loan, forcing banks to liquidate their portfolios to pay their debts.

12 See Davidson (1978), Chapter 4.

Part III
Financial systems

6 Aggregate savings, finance and investment

1 Introduction

It has long been argued that some (or perhaps all) of the central ideas advanced by Keynes in the GT have been either ignored or misunderstood by most of his interpreters. In the two or three decades after World War II most economists considered themselves to be Keynesian. Keynesianism consisted in fact of propositions that were formulated by other economists, frequently in disregard of Keynes's own views. It was widely believed that Modigliani's rigid wages assumption explained the non-neutrality of money, that Hicks was right in stating that liquidity preference and loanable funds theories of the interest rate were complementary rather than alternatives, or that marginal efficiency of capital (actually corrected to become marginal efficiency of investment) was just a fancy name for the old marginal productivity of capital and that the validity of Keynes's emphasis on demand was strictly confined to the short period. Buried in oblivion were the relation between money and uncertainty, Keynes's theory of asset pricing and capital accumulation in Chapter 17 of the GT, the role of expectations and defensive behaviors in causing deficiencies of effective demand and involuntary unemployment, and other ideas that apparently never got a public hearing since few people actually read the GT, and even less read Keynes's clarifications in the debates that followed its publication. No argument from the GT probably suffered a worse fate, however, than the proposed relationship between savings and investment. Even many of Keynes's supporters did not seem to understand fully what, after all, Keynes meant by the statement that they are *always* equal. Some interpreters decided to ignore Keynes's insistence that they have to be equal in value *at any moment* and postulated that investment and savings were equal *only in equilibrium*. This view was usually completed by the notion that the income multiplier was the mechanism through which the equality was to be finally achieved when the economy reached its equilibrium position. Others stated that investment and savings are equal *ex definitione* or, which is a variation of the same idea, that national accounting principles guarantee that they be equal (with changes in inventories being the adjusting variable). Finally, a variation eclectically combining both the preceding arguments seems to argue that *ex post*, but not *ex ante*, investment and savings are always equal.

A large number of the macroeconomic theories presented as Keynesian incorporated one of these interpretations even though Keynes himself explicitly disavowed each and all of them.

The obscurity of the relationship between investment and saving made life easier for those economists intending to restore the "classical" approach, as Keynes called it. If even Keynes's own followers could not agree on what that relationship was after all, why not go back to the familiar view which had been held for so long? In contrast, the strength of the classical argument is certainly due, to a large extent, to its intuitive character. The classical point is in fact simple: how can anyone accumulate capital without putting aside some fraction of one's income to be accumulated as capital? The answer to such a question, of course, and Keynes stressed its agreement more than once, is "one cannot." The point of his criticism and argument is not that investment can be realized without saving also being created, but how do the two variables interact in the capital accumulation process. The classical view is that the *act* of saving has to happen *before* the *act* of investment and is, to some extent, independent of the latter. The divergence between Keynes and the classics relates to the process by which *both* investment and savings emerge, not in the assumption that investment can be done without savings.

What follows, therefore, will focus on the process of investment in "classical" and in Keynes's approaches. In the next section we will examine the classical view, taking Wicksell and his followers of the Stockholm School as its most advanced strand. Section Three will then turn to Keynes's conception of how the investment process works in entrepreneurial (or monetary) economies. Section Four will stress the contrasts between the two approaches. Section Five concludes.

2 The "classical" view of the investment process

The classical[1] approach to capital accumulation relies on the very simple and accessible (and, precisely for this reason, very attractive) theoretical concept of a *corn economy*, an economy where corn is the sole input and output. The concept abstracts from practically every complication one could think of that could be involved in the process of capital accumulation. One conceives an economy which is able not only to provide for its own *necessary* consumption (i.e., the consumption level which allow the simple reproduction of the community) but can actually produce a net output[2] that is higher than what is needed for immediate survival. This society can choose between expanding its current consumption levels or putting aside some fraction of its consumable output to increase production levels in the future. In the corn economy we can describe this choice between consumption and saving for investment without any concern either with the behavior of relative prices (there is only one good, corn, that can be consumed or saved and reinvested in expanding production) or of monetary variables (such as, for instance, money prices of inputs and outputs).

In a corn economy, investment cannot be done unless saving has taken place previously. Members of this economy have to decide to abstain from consumption before they can use the surplus grain to increase the scale of production. Investment cannot be realized without the previous provision of savings, represented by the non-consumed share of the grain output.

The consideration of a *monetary* economy should not change the essential picture of how a corn economy works with respect to saving and investment decisions. The idea still remains that one cannot invest without previously saving some fraction of current income although money (or, more exactly, credit) covers the process with a veil. Classical theorizing along Wicksellian lines aims precisely at piercing this veil.

How does a monetary economy work? To what extent is it different from a pure corn economy? The first difference is obvious: in monetary economies people and firms are paid in money, not in goods, and exchange money for the goods and services they demand. Classical authors, however, did not seem to make much of this point. Surely, the introduction of money makes trade more efficient, but money is considered only in its means-of-payment function, with no impact on the operation of the economy beyond short-term distortions derived from monetary illusion, that is, the confusion between money and real prices that are expected to dissipate in time.[3]

Saving and investing do become a little more complicated though. Now, savers do not transfer corn directly, in kind, to investors. Two concomitant processes have to take place. Savers transfer the purchasing power corresponding to the share of their income they do not want to consume to investors in the form of money. The latter then use it to buy the surplus of goods that was left over after consumption expenditures took place. The monetary process is more indirect, but no substantive difference emerges with respect to a pure corn economy. When savers transfer to investors the money value of their non-spent income, investors are taking hold of precisely the same value of non-consumed output.

Acknowledging the *monetary* form of savings, though, did present some new difficulties. *Real* saving has always been taken to be an unambiguous reference to the non-consumed share of income. But when Wicksell dealt with *monetary* savings he seemed to sometimes confuse *saving some share of monetary income* with *hoarding money*. After observing that hoarding implies withdrawing cash from circulation, he noted that such act could be compensated by somebody else's simultaneous dishoarding "with no effect on money in circulation and prices" (Wicksell 2007: 8). And he went on:

> From the economic point of view of the individual the saving achieves its purpose, since the person saving will at a future date consume what he now forgoes and which somebody else will then forgo. From the social point of view, the only result will be that some part of the supply of money will habitually be withdrawn from circulation; or, as we prefer to express it, that the velocity of circulation of all existing money will be retarded. Again, if anybody adopted the same procedure at the same time, this result would not be

achieved. So long as saving is continued the price of commodities falls, and if everybody saves uniformly, everybody will continue to obtain just as many commodities for their remaining income as if they had not saved and were in fact not compelled to restrict their consumption. But when once the money so accumulated is returned to circulation, the prices of all commodities will rise, and nobody will be able to increase his consumption. Thus saving will not have involved any sacrifice, and the result will prove to be exactly nothing.

(Ibid.: 8–9)

The question was *not* made easier when Wicksell added another difference between barter and monetary economies: the existence of banks. In its simplest functional definition, a bank is an institution that accepts deposits from the public to use them to make loans to borrowers. Banks were conceived thus as financial *intermediaries*, standing between savers, who could choose the type and volume of deposits they want, and investors, who would borrow from the bank.[4] Savers and investors were assumed to be the main, if not necessarily the sole, suppliers and demanders of resources to and from the bank.

Of course, formally, deposits are just a specific modality of *loans* made to banks. As in the case of other types of loans, banks commit to return the value deposited with them under specified conditions. Demand deposits offer full liquidity, being redeemable in currency on demand by depositors. Time deposits establish some minimum investment period and compensate for it by paying a higher interest rate than demand deposits (which usually, but not necessarily, pay zero rates of interest). With the resources collected from depositors, so the story goes, banks can buy assets, such as debt contracts from borrowing firms.

Banks further complicated and made more opaque the relationship between saving and investment but again they were not allowed to change its ultimate nature. Bank deposits and loans dealt with the *means to purchase* the goods that are going to be accumulated. The possibility of accumulation continued to depend on the desire of income earners to save and of investors to invest. The existence of credit institutions could not change that basic reality. One way to deal with the possibility of divergent behaviors of savers and investors, on the one hand, and banks, on the other, was to constrain bank activity to play strictly the role of intermediation between savers and investors, so that the value of loans corresponds exactly to the value of savings. This can only be done, however, at a potentially high price. One has to assume, first, that savers deposit in banks all their savings and nothing but their savings. Unless this condition is fulfilled, total savings and loanable funds will differ in value. The second condition is that credit supply offered by banks is funded entirely by savings deposits.

The first condition is problematic for two reasons. First, savers may use themselves some fraction of their savings to finance directly their own or other people's investments. Retained profits are the most important source of funds for investment practically everywhere. Credit can only capture the fraction of savings that will be shifted from savers to (different) investors. Second, and more relevant, banks are not only, and perhaps not even mainly, credit providers anymore. In modern monetary economies, banks are providers of payment system services. The public hold *transaction* deposits in banks as well as *idle* deposits that could represent some sort of saving. Frequently both types of deposits are maintained in the *same* accounts. For banks no essential difference exists between transaction deposits and saving deposits, both being recognized as "sources" of loanable funds, which means that banks lend transactional balances as well as "saving" deposits, violating the second condition for equivalence of total savings and the supply of loanable funds.

Bertil Ohlin, one of the pillars of the Stockholm School, maintained that the savings supply function, that is, "planned" savings, was the ultimate determinant of the supply of credit, and the same happened to planned investments and the demand for credit, despite some discrepancies that could blur the fundamental equivalence between them:

> The relation between the curves referring to savings and investment and those referring to credit is close should be obvious. If a man plans to save, must he not either plan to invest or to lend? Will not, then, the planned supply of credit be equal to the planned savings, if the use of one's own savings for new investment if treated as giving credit to oneself? No, not quite. It is possible to plan to save and to increase the quantity of cash instead of lending. Also one can plan to extend new credit in excess of planned savings, if own is willing to reduce one's own quantity of cash. Besides, one can plan to extend credit instead of reinvesting "capital made free," i.e. "depreciation money." Similarly with the planned demand for credit, which may differ from planned new investment owing to a desire to vary the cash held, to cover expected losses or to finance consumption. But this is only one side of the difference. The other one is that one may plan to take credit for the purchase of old assets, i.e. for financial investment. This has nothing to do with the new investment of the industrial sphere, which is related to savings. One may also plan "financial disinvestment," e.g. through the sale of a house, and plan to use the proceeds to extend new credit, e.g. to the man who buys the house. Thirdly, the banking system may plan to increase or reduce the volume of credit. Evidently, the curves of demand and supply of credit, which are identical with the curves of supply and demand for claims, are quite different from but interrelated with the curves which refer to planned new investment and savings.[5]
>
> (Ohlin 1937: 425)

Others seemed to hold savings and bank loans as alternatives rather than transformations of one another. Dennis Robertson, for example, listed the supply of loanable funds as consisting of:

1 current savings;
2 "disentangling," that is, past savings currently released as depreciation or working capital;

3   net dishoardings; and
4   net bank loans (Robertson 1988: 3).[6]

Robertson and, of course, Wicksell himself, moreover, realized that, when supplying credit, banks not only were not necessarily constrained by the amount of savings deposits the public desired to hold but that they could actually *create* credit, given the special nature of their liabilities. Robertson (1988: 41) acknowledged that:

> ... bank-money comes into existence mainly as the result of loans and investment made by the banking system, and that consequently, in most circumstances, the proximate forces determining its amount is a series of decisions made by some person or persons situated within the banking system.[7]

Robertson, however, maintained, without explanation, that:

> The real value of a country's bank-money is the same thing as the amount of real savings which the public has put in the past at the disposal of industry through the medium of the banks, and its amount lies in the discretion of the public and not of the banks.
>
> (Ibid.: 42)

Wicksell explicitly recognized the potentially disturbing implications of acknowledging the ability of banks to multiply their liabilities. In this approach, possible divergences between savings and credit were a serious threat to macroeconomic equilibrium.[8]

Money and credit, therefore, made trades more efficient but credit caused the money veil to become thicker. To save a fraction of one's income was to subtract from money circulation by acquiring a bank deposit. However, the bank could put the value of the deposit back into monetary circulation by making a loan. Savings were increased but monetary circulation was intact. A Wicksellian puzzle emerged: should prices go down because savings were increased or stand still because monetary circulation remained the same?

Moreover, the operation of banks allowed the supply of bank credit to diverge from the underlying supply of savings, creating the possibility of new types of imbalances in the economy. These imbalances would be manifest in the possibility that the *natural* rate of interest (that made saving and investment equal) could be different from the *market* rate of interest (that made supply of and demand for credit equal). Of course, all these dilemmas could be avoided if the conditions for the equality of aggregate savings and financial savings could be guaranteed. For our purposes, this means that the classical approach contained a fundamental *normative* view of what should be the "correct" role of banks: in order to minimize imbalances in the economy, they should act essentially as *pure intermediaries* between ultimate savers and investors.

3 Keynes on saving and investment

In *A Treatise on Money*, published in 1930, Keynes presented his personal view of Wicksell's theory of the interest rate, based on definitions of saving and investment that sharply contrasted with the definitions he proposed later, in the GT. In the *Treatise*, as he had done before, in his *Tract on Monetary Reform*, Keynes did not question the fundamental truth of classical theory. The argument relied on the interplay of two independent functions, saving and investment, meant to represent planned *saving* and *planned* investment. In fact, Keynes argued that this was the only definition that made sense, since otherwise they would always be equal in value:

> My definition of *income* is thought paradoxical because I excluded from it
> [...] windfall profits and losses, and my definition of *saving*, being the
> excess of income thus defined over expenditure on consumption, corres-
> ponds to my definition of *income*. But those who object to those definitions
> have not, I think, followed out to the end the consequences of rejecting
> them. For if windfall profits and losses are included in income, [...] and
> saving as the excess of income thus defined over expenditure on consump-
> tion, it follows that saving is in all cases exactly equal to the value of current
> investment. That is to say the total volume of saving ceases to be a factor
> having any independent existence. Its amount cannot be affected by the vol-
> untary decision of the various recipients of income as to how much of their
> income they will spend on consumption; and it solely depends on what the
> value of current investment happens to be.
>
> (CW 5: xxiii)

Naturally, a forward-looking concept of planned saving could only relate to *expected* income. But what if expected income turned out different from realized income? How would *actual* saving behave? To deal with this problem, Keynes suggested that these unexpected changes in income should be treated separately, as windfall gains or losses, since, being unexpected at the moment of decision, they could not have influenced it.

Keynes seemed unsure, however, of what role, if any, should be given to these unexpected, ex post gains and losses. Keynes's choice, expressed in the famous widow's cruse argument, was the target of heavy criticism because it failed to respect the most obvious point of contrast between planned savings and windfall gains, that is, their asynchrony. Keynes decided to abandon any concept of saving that could depend on the notion of *expected* income (and actually used the difficulties he met with the concept against Ohlin in the 1937 The Economic Journal debate reported here).

In the interval between the publication of the *Treatise* and the publication of the GT, Keynes's views on how a modern entrepreneurial economy works underwent a profound change. The most important change happened not so much with respect to individual concepts and theoretical instruments, but at the more abstract level of how a modern monetary economy works, as seen in Chapter 1. In this new setting, the relationship between investment and saving changed dramatically, leaving behind the corn economy of the classical economists, even in its more modern Wicksellian embodiment.

To shortly describe the new view, in a monetary economy, a person planning an investment has two concerns. First, it is necessary to get hold of *money* to buy the goods that constitute the investment. This is *demand for money to buy (capital) goods*, no different in character from the transactional demand for money. Keynes called it the *finance motive to demand money* when he introduced the idea in the debate with Ohlin. The language used by Keynes in this exchange may have been somewhat unfortunate, however. The use of the term *finance* contributed to add some confusion to an already convoluted conversation. The meaning of finance in this context remained very obscure to the participants in the debate until the very end of their exchange, when Keynes finally clarified the meaning he gave to the concept. The finance motive to demand money was initially introduced by Keynes through an analogy with saving that was, at the very least, exceedingly ambiguous in the context of the debate:

> Planned investment – i.e. investment ex-ante – may have to secure its "financial provision" before the investment takes place; that is to say, before the corresponding saving has taken place. It is, so to speak, as though a particular piece of saving had to be earmarked against a particular piece of investment before either has occurred, before it is known who is going to do the saving himself. There has, therefore, to be a technique to bridge this gap between the time when the decision to invest is taken and the time when the correlative investment and saving actually occur.
>
> (CW 14: 246)

Keynes presented his views much more clearly elsewhere:

> The rate of interest is determined by the total demand and total supply of cash or liquid resources. The total demand falls into two parts: the inactive demand due to the state of confidence and expectation on the part of the owners of wealth, and the active demand due to the level of activity established by the decisions of the entrepreneurs. *The active demand in its turn falls into two parts: the demand due to the time lag between the inception and the execution of the entrepreneur's decisions, and the part due to the time lags between the receipt and the disposal of income by the public and also between the receipt by entrepreneurs of their sale proceeds and the payment by them of wages, etc. An increase in activity raises the demand for cash, first of all to provide for the first of these time lags in circulation, and then to provide for the second of them.* Thereafter the demand for cash falls away unless the completed activity is being succeeded by a new activity. A given stock of cash provides a revolving fund for a steady flow of activity; but an increased rate of flow needs an increased stock to keep the channels

filled. When decisions are made which will lead to an increase in activity, the effect is first felt in the demand for more cash or "finance."

(CW 14: 230, my emphasis)

The finance motive to demand money may be satisfied by a number of sources: retained profits accumulated as bank deposits, bank loans and overdrafts, placement of securities, etc. because there could be some idle liquidity in some points of monetary circulation. But, Keynes insisted, it is *money*, not saving, that is the object of demand.

The entrepreneur's second concern relates to the *funding* for this investment, that is, the issuance of permanent obligations to support holding the newly-acquired assets in his balance sheet (Keynes 1937: 40). Although Keynes dedicated very little space to this during the debate with Ohlin, he did develop the idea later, when discussing the ideal timing for funding *government* spending during the war. Then, the point was to determine when public debt securities should be placed to cover those expenditures. Keynes did not enter into any details related to funding modalities, it was the *timing* of funding operations that mattered to him. Discretionary spending (government expenditures as much as investment spending) creates income, directly and through the multiplier effect. Rising incomes generate rising savings in search of wealth accumulation vehicles. Funding of deficit spending should be timed to coincide with the full operation of the multiplier. Thus, the lag between making the expenditure and the placement of long-term securities

> must also be long enough in point of time for the new savings to reach the ultimate holder, who alone is in a position to embark them in a permanent investment, and to allow him to make an unhurried decision.
>
> (CW 21: 543)

There still remained the problem of how the ultimate holders' demand for assets will be divided among the several classes of assets, which depends on the public's liquidity preferences, as has been explained in the preceding chapters. In Keynes's approach, shaping the supply of assets according to the liquidity preferences of buyers is one of the main functions of the financial system.[9]

There are, therefore, three dimensions to the investment process. First, there is a monetary dimension. Investing means *acquiring* goods of a special nature, and, as it is the case of any act of spending, the buyer of investment goods needs to get hold of money to do it. This is what Keynes called "finance."[10] It is thus a problem of monetary circulation, that is, whether there is sufficient *liquidity* in the economy to allow discretionary expenditures to take place without pushing the interest rate upwards.[11]

Second, there is the goods market dimension. For an investment to be realized it is necessary that non-consumable output is made available. To save is actually to release goods, labor and means of production to be used as investment.[12] *Keynes argued insistently that there can be no investment without the concomitant generation of savings.*

Saving, however, is created *at the same time* in which investment takes place, not before, in contrast to what happens in the corn economy, because investments is the value of the total expenditure in excess of consumption expenditures, while saving is constituted by goods and services that are made available for this investment, consisting of the excess of total output over the goods purchased for consumption purposes. This is why investment and saving are *always* equal, not because they are two different names for the same thing nor because this is a result of some definitional artifice or accounting practice.[13] The difference with the classics is, first, the *sequence* through which the investment process develops, beginning in the money market so that the investment *expenditure* can be made, which causes the corresponding saving to come into existence as investment goods are produced to satisfy the demand; second, the acknowledgement that saving can be increased either by reducing consumption expenditures (when the economy is in full employment) *or by increasing income* (*when there is involuntary unemployment*).[14] Of course, the second alternative did not exist in the classical world of Say's law.

There is finally a third dimension, the financial dimension. To save is not only to refrain from consumption, releasing goods, labor and means of production, but it is also to demand assets. As Keynes stated it (CW 7: 166), once a person decides how much of his or her income will be spent on consumption (and therefore how much will be saved), he or she still has to decide in which form the saving will be stored, choosing among the available classes of assets. The saver may be able, for instance, to keep non-consumed income in the form of liquid assets, buying liquid financial assets issued by banking institutions, or less liquid assets sold by other financial and non-financial institutions. Savers, therefore, will make their wealth accumulation decisions in accordance with their *liquidity preferences*.

Thus, the investment process in a monetary or entrepreneurial economy follows a very different timeline than that conceived by classical economists. Keynes emphasized that making investment *expenditures* requires money, not income or saving, to be made available to investors.[15] Banks, however, are also important to Ohlin's Stockholm School narrative of the Wicksellian classical approach. At the end of the day, the real points of contention between Keynes and Wicksellians are three: first, whether banks intervene in this process because they supply money (by creating deposits) or credit (by extending loans); second, if the input banks need to do their job is monetary reserves or ex-ante, desired saving; and, third, whether income (or saving) is fixed or variable. Keynes's answered to these queries that banks' role in the investment process is to supply money by creating deposits on the basis of a given level of reserves. In addition, total income was determined by expenditure. Ohlin's answer is that banks supply credit fed by the deposits originated by desired savings. His view on income determination, on the other hand, was not entirely clear, although Wicksell's was: expenditure determines *nominal* income, but cannot affect *real* income.

4 Contrasts between the two approaches

At a fundamental level, the main bone of contention between Keynes's and Wicksell's theoretical approaches boils down to their different concepts of monetary economy. While Wicksell seemed to have considered a monetary economy a *modified form* of a barter economy,[16] Keynes considered monetary economies to be an entirely different social arrangement, where production and capital accumulation are pursued by firms motivated by the expectations of money profit, as explained in Chapter 1.

Keynes considered firms to be much more than mere groupings of consumers joining their factor- of-production services to exploit some possible increasing returns from collective methods of production. Firms and entrepreneurs have an objective function of their own, not reducible to individuals deriving satisfaction from consuming goods. As Keynes put it:

> An entrepreneur is interested, not in the amount of product, but in the amount of *money* which will fall to his share. He will increase his output if by so doing he expects to increase his money profit, even though this profit represents a smaller quantity of product than before. The explanation for this is evident. The employment of factors of production to increase output involves the entrepreneur in the disbursement, not of product, but of money.
>
> (CW 29: 82, Keynes's emphasis)

In fact, not only firms, but individuals too are supposed to prefer the accumulation of wealth in monetary form, as explained by liquidity preference theory. In such economies, everybody's prime consideration is ensuring the *liquidity* of their assets.

As explained by Paul Davidson (2002: 7), "in Keynes's scheme of things, real world financial markets provide liquidity and not necessarily efficiency," while for "the classical scheme, free financial markets are the efficient allocator of capital goods that promotes the economic progress of society." Liquidity is provided in two ways:

1 banks *create* liquidity, by creating deposits when buying assets from the public, for instance, when a loan if conceded to firms and individuals, because banks' deposit liabilities are generally accepted as means of payment;
2 non-banking financial institutions *intermediate* liquidity by finding in the economy liquidity-holders willing to trade liquid for non-liquid assets in exchange for a reward in the form of an interest rate. (Cardim de Carvalho and Kregel 2010).

The ability of banks to *create* finance radically separates Keynes and the Classics. "Keynesian" banks can create finance because their liabilities are accepted as means of payment. They are not bound by whatever value depositors wanted to lend them previously.[17] They actually create deposits as they lend, in a purely bookkeeping operation. The only constraints on banks' decision to lend, that is, to issue deposit liabilities to the credit of borrowers, are the availability or access to reserves and their own liquidity preferences.

Banks in the classical world, in contrast, do not create funds, they can only intermediate resources given up by savers. As stated by Gurley and Shaw (1955)'s paradigmatic presentation, financial institutions capture financial resources from surplus units (those who plan to spend, in consumption and real investment, less than their current income) and transfer them to deficit units (those planning to spend more than their current income). Banks are, thus, no different from other intermediaries:

> We take exception to the view that banks stand apart in their ability to create loanable funds out of hand, while other intermediaries in contrast are busy with the modest brokerage function of transmitting loanable funds that are somehow generated elsewhere. Neither banks not other intermediaries create loanable funds. That is the prerogative of spending units with surpluses on income and product account.
>
> (Gurley and Shaw 1955: 521)

Wicksell, on the other hand, recognizes that banks can multiply *credit*, but this is not an element of the *normal* dynamics of monetary economies. If banks do extend credit beyond the value of desired savings, inflation will ensue because banks can extend credit but cannot guarantee the availability of goods and services to attend the increased demand supported by that credit. In equilibrium, banks should be neutral, that is, the market rate of interest should be equal to the natural rate of interest. It is interesting to notice that the divergence between the two rates, and the possibility of cumulative disequilibria, emerging from the operation of banks, which interested Wicksell very much, is not even mentioned by Ohlin in his summary of the arguments of the Stockholm School. The apparent contradiction between Gurley and Shaw, on the one hand, and Wicksell dissolves when one realizes that they are in fact saying exactly the same thing: that financial systems can create *credit*, but not *loanable funds*, because loanable funds are nothing but the value of people's desired savings, not of actual loans. As Gurley and Shaw (1955: 522) added, banks and non-banks "are loanable-funds brokers. Both create credit." Of course, if the expression "loanable funds" is proposed as no more than another *name* for savings one can justly wonder what is gained by using it.

Keynes's opposition to the classical approach was thus wholesale. The narrative of investment/saving link in each theory was based on a dramatically different view of how the economy is structured and operates. In particular, the roles played by money and finance in each approach simply cannot be reconciled.

Keynes also added some more specific topical criticisms of the Stockholm School, as described by Ohlin in their 1937 The Economic Journal exchange. In particular, Keynes took exception of the concept of ex-ante or planned savings.[18] According to Keynes, such a variable is not observable and do not result in any observable behavior or market result. One cannot demand assets with ex-ante savings, one cannot deposit desired savings. In Keynes's words, "the ex-ante saver has no cash, but it is cash that the ex-ante investor requires" (Keynes 1937: 665–666).

Moreover, Ohlin's banks seem to receive only savings deposits, while Keynes's bank receives both transaction deposits and savings deposits. In other words, Keynes acknowledges that the public does not maintain as deposits only the value which they don't intend to spend, but in fact most of the purchasing power they want to keep in liquid form, for performing transactions *and* to accumulate as savings. Therefore, the bank does not lend only desired *savings*, but all resources it can put its hands on.[19]

The central point, therefore, is that what matters for investment is neither realized savings nor, in fact, ex ante or desired savings. Banks, not savers, are the suppliers of the liquidity that the investor needs to order investment goods. The classical bank depends on savers to make deposits. The Keynesian bank creates deposits when it buys assets. The funds are spent generating income out of which the necessary saving is realized. Wicksell, as we saw, recognized that banks may multiply deposits but saw it as a fundamentally disruptive possibility enhancing the possibility that self-amplifying disequilibria emerge. Keynes know that such disequilibria might actually emerge, but only when full employment prevailed.

5 Conclusion

The persistence of classical ideas on the relation between saving and investment so many decades after the publication of the GT bears witness to the power of their appeal not only for the general public but also to economists, who perhaps should know better. In fact, that so many economists still think that saving is a pre-condition to investment, just as it was in the corn economy, bears witness also to the difficulty of understanding how modern economies work. Of course, the persistence of the corn economy model of thought is also responsible for the correlated ideas that an economy, like a family, has to live within its means and that austerity is the right recipe to deal with debt overhangs.

Keynes's proposition that investment creates saving sounds to many people the same as saying that capital can be created out of nothing. Keynes fought this notion, and even wrote in the GT that he considered the notion entertained by classical economists according to which no investment can be realized without savings a lesser mistake compared to "magical" propositions of the type "investment can prescind of savings" (CW 7: 83). Capitalism does no magic. Keynes's point is that modern economies work according to their own logic, subject to different constraints, with agents being moved by different stimuli in comparison with a corn economy. Monetary economies seldom operate at full employment, and because of that investments may not need a previous decision to save in order to release real resources from consumption. Investment and consumption actually move together in these economies, except at full employment. To achieve a proper understanding of such mechanisms was the point of creating the concept of an entrepreneurial or monetary economy.

The contrast between Keynes and the classics on the matter of investment and saving, therefore, is not a question of defining the terms differently but of fitting them in different narratives. In Keynes's monetary economy, when a decision to invest is made, the investor has to get hold of money to buy the desired investment goods. It is in the money circulation that this demand is accommodated, through the satisfaction of what he called the finance motive to demand money. Once the investor is in possession of the necessary amount of money he orders those goods. The producer of investment goods sets in motion the process of production in which those goods will come into existence, and the corresponding income will be appropriated by the owners of factors of production. At this moment, investment is no longer a plan, but a reality and, at the same time, "real" saving, in the form of non-consumable output, comes into existence too. The owners of factors of production will then use some fraction of their higher income to increase their own consumption raising output and income again and again, until this multiplication process is exhausted. At this point, there will be a demand for assets, i.e., financial savings, that is of the same total value as the original investment. This is the proper moment for public and private investors to fund the obligations incurred to allow the investment expenditures.

From this point of view, criticizing the classical view and its implications in terms of economic policy cannot circumvent the need to substitute the narrative of a monetary economy for the intuitive corn economy model that still dominates economic thought. As suggested in the chapter, a crucial step to be emphasized in the new narrative is the assumption that in monetary economies output levels (and employment) are decided on the basis of the expectations of demand of businessmen and that banks are capable of creating the liquidity that can satisfy the demand for money that initiates the process. This is the obvious starting point of Keynesian criticisms of the macroeconomic policies pursued after the financial crisis of 2007–2008 in the United States and, most intensely, in the European Union. *Decreasing* incomes cannot generate *increasing* savings except at the cost of disproportional sacrifices. Saving releases resources, but releasing resources when there is already a large number of unemployed workers and means of production is a waste, pure and simple. To expect that increasing waste and decreasing income will increase lenders' confidence is to mistake religious faith for the analysis of businessmen's motives.

In sum, finance, from a Keynesian perspective, is therefore a far more complex function than merely intermediating saving or capital. Finance creates *and* distributes liquidity. Investment, like consumption, relies on the possibility of paying for the desired goods, so an appropriate rendition of how investment comes into existence requires a proper understanding (including measurement) of how finance is created and allocated. Investment financing will be related, of course, to aggregate saving, since investment and saving are equal. Before examining if investment financing is being adequately provided, however, it is essential that a proper knowledge of how the financial (including the banking) system is structured and how its segments are articulated to one another be obtained.

Notes

1 More than ever it is important to stress again that we use the term "classical" in this book in the same sense which Keynes introduced it in the GT, given that capital accumulation was the main focus of the Classical Political Economy of Smith, Ricardo and others, which most people associate with the term *classical*. Nowadays, Keynes's usage is widely considered inadequate. The expression *neoclassical* would be preferred by some, although it could be argued that this label covers a much larger group of theoretical approaches to the problems that interested Keynes. Be it as it may, the reader is alerted to the specific meaning of the word in this book.

2 Net of the utilization of corn as seeds necessary to reproduce the same output of corn in the next period.

3 Marx was one of the few economists to realize that even as a mere means of payment money could change the dynamics of a market economy. According to Marx (1978: 502, 515), the use of money as an intermediary of trades created what he called a "general possibility of crisis," since the seller of goods for money could retain it instead of spending it, interrupting the "commodity cycle," that is, the sequence of purchase of raw materials and labor force, production of goods, and their sale to use the proceeds to reinitiate the process. However, Marx also argued that while this created the *possibility* of crises, it was not enough to provide an actual explanation of crises.

4 Modern neoclassical economists maintain the view that "[b]anks collect savings from depositors and lend the funds to firms and households" (Strahan 2010: 112). Gorton and Winton (2002) defined "bank-like" intermediaries as

> firms with the following characteristics: 1. They borrow from one group of agents and lend to another group of agents. 2. The borrowing and lending groups are large, suggesting diversification on each side of the balance sheet. 3. The claims issued to borrowers and to lender have different state contingent payoffs. The terms "borrow" and "lend" mean that the contracts involved are debt contracts.

5 Myrdal (1965: 109–112) tried to describe the relation between saving and credit but ended up with a proposition where any result is possible depending on which ad hoc assumptions are chosen as to bank preferences.

6 Demand for loanable funds includes the same items, with their signs changed.

7

> The discovery that money deposited on a guarantee to repay on demand could be partially loaned without endangering the liquidity of the institution in question constituted, however, an important advance in banking technique, which in its turn led to the discovery of the credit note. For just as simply as deposits of money were accepted against a certificate of deposit and were then lent out to others, whilst the certificate of deposit might continue to be used by the owner as a medium of payment and be transferred to others, so also certificates of deposit might be issued against ample security to persons who had *not* deposited any money in the bank.
>
> (Wicksell 2007: 76)

8 Wicksell tried to attenuate this threat, however, by postulating again a different behavior to saving deposits in comparison to demand deposits: "On the other hand, the difference is great between deposits which are based on money saved, and are therefore intended for long date capitalization, and those deposits which consist of occasional surpluses of bank credits" (Wicksell 2007: 86). He seemed to imply that banks would be more parsimonious in supplying credit funded by savings deposits than of demand deposits.

9 The preferences of buyers of financial assets should express themselves in yield curves, the curves relating rates of interest and characteristics of financial assets (most

commonly maturities, but that can also describe preferences in terms of other characteristics such as whether debt is public or private or whether the securities are liquid or not). Yield curves, on the other hand, inform issuers of securities of the public's preferences helping them to shape their own balance sheet strategies. It is in this particular issue that Hyman Minsky made his most important contributions to the development of Keynes's liquidity preference theory.

10　The peculiar sense in which Keynes used the term *finance* gave rise to some confusion not only in his own debates with contemporaries but also among later generations of Keynesian economists and their opponents, particularly those defending loanables funds theories. Keynes clarified the meaning he attributed to the term finance in his final contribution to the debate with Ohlin, Robertson and Hawtrey, in *The Economic Journal* on the relationship between saving and investment:

> A large part of the outstanding confusion is due, I think, to Mr. Robertson's thinking of "finance" as consisting in bank loans; whereas in the article under discussion I introduced this term to mean the *cash* temporarily held by entrepreneurs to provide against the outgoings in respect of an impending new activity.
>
> (CW 14: 229)

Kalecki, usually less concerned with the niceties of the classical approach, makes investors go directly to the central bank to obtain finance, which may or may not make the point clearer (Kalecki 1971).

11　In Chapter 4 we argued that how liquidity is supplied, and under which constraints, is not explored in the GT.

12

> For the object of saving is to release labor for employment on producing capital-goods such as houses, factories, roads, machines, and the like. But if there is a large unemployed surplus already available for such purposes, then the effect of saving is merely add to this surplus and therefore to increase the number of the unemployed.
>
> (Keynes 1963: 151)

13

> The equivalence between the quantity of saving and the quantity of investment emerges from the bilateral character of the transactions between the producer on the one hand and, in the other hand, the consumer or the purchases of capital equipment.
>
> (CW 7: 63)

A similar equality is verified in the assets market: "But no one can save without acquiring an asset which he did not previously possess, unless *either* an asset of equal value is newly produced *or* someone else parts with an asset of that value which he previously had" (ibid.: 81–82).

14

> The reconciliation of the identity between saving and investment with the apparent "free-will" of the individual to save what he chooses irrespective of what he or others may be investing, essentially, depends on saving being, like spending, a two-sided affair [...]. Every such attempt to save more by reducing consumption will so affect incomes that the attempt necessarily defeats itself. It is, of course, just as impossible for the community as a whole to save less than the amount of current investment, since the attempt to do so will necessarily raise incomes to a level at which the sums which individuals choose do save add up to a figure exactly equal to the amount of investment.
>
> (CW 7: 84)

15

> The transition from a lower to a higher scale of activity involves an increased demand for liquid resources which cannot be met without a rise in the rate of interest, unless the banks are ready to lend more cash or the rest of the public to release more cash at the existing rate of interest. If there is no change in the liquidity position, the public can save ex-ante and ex-post and ex-anything-else until they are blue in the face, without alleviating the problem in the least – unless, indeed, the result of their efforts is to lower the scale of activity to what was before.
>
> (Keynes 1937: 668)

16 To be fair, Wicksell (2007: 6) did warn against taking his view too far:

> Naturally, however, our simplification is only provisional. Economists frequently go too far when they assume that the economic laws which they have deduced on barter assumptions may be applied without qualification of actual conditions, in which money actually affects practically all exchanges and investments or transfers of capital.

As noted in Chapter 1, Keynes was very forceful on this point: "The idea that it is comparatively easy to adapt the hypothetical conclusions of a real-wage [barter] economics to the real world of monetary economics is a mistake" (CW 13: 410).

17 See the exchange between Keynes, Reginald McKenna and R. Brand during a session of the Macmillan Committee, already referred to (CW 20: 87–89). For the latitude of banks when creating liabilities, see the historical and theoretical exploration made by Kregel (1998).

18 As also did Robertson (1988: 7).

19 Again, in his Wicksellian analysis in the *Treatise on Money*, Keynes did try to segregate transaction deposits from saving deposits in banking data, not very successfully. In the GT he abandoned the distinction.

7 Financial fragility and systemic crises

1 Introduction

Liquidity Preference theory branched out into a number of fields, among which one counts the analysis of financial fragility processes and financial crises. These developments became especially important once the world economy got in 2007 into the worst turbulence it has experienced since the 1930s.

The preceding chapter presented the discussion of how Keynesian liquidity preference theory allows the articulation of monetary and financial factors to create a unified approach to investment and capital accumulation. Entrepreneurs need to have access to money, not savings, whether real or financial, ex ante or ex post, or of any other type, to effect the intended spending in investment goods. In monetary or entrepreneurial economies, financing investment is, first of all, a money market problem, solving the question of how to give access to would-be investors to the money they need to buy those goods.

But we saw that accessing money is only the first step in the investment process. Building a solvent and liquid balance sheet is the next problem to be attacked by investing entrepreneurs, especially those who are conscious of the uncertainties that surround the future and the risks real investment exposes them to. However, safer balance sheet strategies are costly which may induce some investors to make riskier bets than they would otherwise prefer. Moreover, if a certain number of investors turn out to be unable to honor their obligations, this may end up threatening the whole financial system, and, perhaps, the whole economy. The risk of amplification of individual or local difficulties into a full-fledged crisis is what is called *systemic risk*.

The financial crisis that began in the United States in early 2007 and has subsequently spread to the rest of the world has reawakened interest on the concept of systemic risk. As the depth and reach of the current crisis has become more and more clear to all, a new consensus seems to be forming. It is increasingly accepted that regulation failures bear most of the responsibility for the current financial collapse. For some, the financial liberalization process initiated in the 1980s is to blame. In particular, the *privatization* of financial regulation, that is, the increasing reliance on self-regulation by the financial industry and on market discipline is seen to have failed to strengthen systemic stability. In the opposite corner, it is argued that insufficient reliance on market discipline is the real culprit of the crisis. Given the dominance of the liberalizing party in the last thirty years, however, the pendulum moved toward a more interventionist posture, although much of the early enthusiasm of government authorities for new measures to curb speculative excesses of financial institutions seems to have vanished later.

Nevertheless, as remarked by Allen and Gale (2006: 3), "financial regulation should be based on a careful analysis of the market failure that justifies government intervention (...)." The definition of financial regulation strategies directed at safeguarding systemic stability has to result from a clear view of the threats to stability. What is a systemic crisis? What may cause it? These are fundamental questions that precede the final and decisive one: how can it be prevented?

One might expect that a generally-accepted concept of systemic crisis should be established at this point in time. Surprisingly, it is not. The characteristics that define a phenomenon as a systemic crisis are not in fact consensual. Nevertheless, one cannot impose efficient prudential regulation to prevent events which cannot be identified. Efficient regulation can only result from holding a clear concept of what the problem one wants to prevent is.

In part, the problem is that systemic crises are rare events and, as a result, not many people are willing to dedicate much effort to seriously research them. But also the problem may be partly ascribed to the intense financial innovation that marked the last thirty years. The notion of systemic crisis grew out of the analysis of the great depression of the 1930s and the features that were believed to characterize that particular chain of events. However, the causes of what happened in the 1930s, which could explain the depth and spread of the crisis, still remain the subject of intense controversy.[1] On the other hand, schools of economic thought that rely on the efficient market hypothesis or believe in the empirical validity of stable equilibrium models are only able to recognize small disequilibria, in the vicinity of equilibrium positions. Systemic crises, for them, can only be the result of huge adverse shocks (like wrong monetary policy decisions) hitting a financial system already distorted and therefore weakened by financial regulation itself or other forms of intervention in the operation of markets. Large-scale coordination failures just can't happen when markets are free to operate efficiently.

Post Keynesians, and some other strands of Keynesian thought, in contrast, are much more comfortable to deal with the concept of systemic crisis. These crises are not expected to be a *normal* feature of modern capitalist economies. They are, however, an ever-present possibility, to be prevented by a combination of financial regulation and proper macroeconomic policies. To develop these propositions, this chapter begins, in Section 2, by examining the recent debate on the nature of systemic crises among mainstream economists, government officials and financial regulators. In particular, we show how the pre-crisis regulatory strategy, which we shall refer as the Basel Strategy, followed from this approach and suffered from its shortcomings. Section 3 presents an alternative Post Keynesian perspective, inspired, of course, by Keynes but also, and prominently, by Hyman Minsky. Section 4 concludes the chapter by drawing some implications from the preceding section to the definition of an alternative regulatory strategy to deal with systemic risks.

2 Emergence and development of the concept of systemic crisis

Antecedents

The notion, but not the term, of systemic risk seems to be originally rooted in Bagehot's (1994) description of a bank panic in Chapter 2 of his book *Lombard Street*. Bagehot presented a bank run as a three-stage process, where initial alarm is transformed into panic and panic into madness, as clients find out that they are unable to borrow what they expect from banks (Bagehot 1994: 28). The first stage of the crisis, alarm, happens when a few *merchants* begin to wonder if they can get enough credit from banks as they are used to, because of rumors about their (or their banks') financial health (Bagehot 1994: 24–25). Panic ensues when that suspicion spreads out and a growing number of merchants

> come to their banker and offer bills for discount, which commonly they would not have offered for days or weeks to come. And if the merchant be a regular customer, a banker does not like to refuse, because if he does he will be said, or may be said, to be in want of money, and so may attract the panic to himself.
>
> (Bagehot 1994: 25)

According to Bagehot,

> [t]he problem of managing a panic must not be thought of as mainly a "banking" problem. It is primarily a mercantile one. (...) all merchants are dependent on borrowing money, and large merchants are dependent on borrowing much money.
>
> (Bagehot 1994: 26)

Banks, that is, the

> holders of the cash reserve must be ready not only to keep it for their own liabilities, but to advance it most freely for the liabilities of others. They must lend to merchants, to minor bankers, to "this man and that man," whenever the security is good. *In wild periods of alarm, one failure makes many, and the best way to prevent the derivative failures is to arrest the primary failure which causes them.*
>
> (Bagehot 1994: 26, my emphasis)

In order for banks to avoid *attracting the panic to themselves*, they have to make cash available, though at higher interest rates and against good security. But this is possible only when the holder of the final reserves lend freely. Otherwise, "[a] ny notion that money is not to be had, or that it may not be had at any price, only raises alarm to panic and enhances panic to madness". (Bagehot 1994: 28)

As we can see, the broad lines of one of the most influential notions of systemic risk were in fact already set by Bagehot. First, the idea that a crisis may begin for purely *psychological* reasons, a bout of possibly groundless suspicion about the financial health of some firms, which may prevent them from getting credit, or creates the suspicion that credit will become scarce. Second, that a crisis spreads because other people may be unable to determine whether they are exposed to the same risk so they try to anticipate their credit demands to avoid contagion. Third, the pressure moves to the banks to which these additional credit demands are directed, depleting their cash reserves. Fourth, the unwillingness or the inability of banks to satisfy these demands may transform panic into madness, a state that is not defined by Bagehot, but the very choice of words seems to express his view clearly enough. Finally, the proposition that panic can be stopped at its first stages by lending freely at penalty interest rates and assuring that money is to be had, although at high interest rates.

All these factors, plus some, will be present in the most popular stylizations of what is supposed to have happened in the great depression of the 1930s, where the concept of systemic crisis is more immediately rooted. The generally accepted stylization runs as follows: after almost a decade of speculative excesses, the US economy was hit by a powerful shock represented by the stock exchange crash of 1929. The stock exchange collapse *per se*, dramatic as it was, could not explain the depression but it served to shake the confidence of the public in the banking system. Universal banks were allowed in the US at that time. Banks which got involved in the speculative adventures of the late 1920s in the securities markets were weakened by the crash. Some of them actually failed, raising the suspicion that others would follow. Fear of losing their deposits led the clients of surviving banks to try to cash them, triggering runs which led even healthy banks to bankruptcy. As a result, the stock of means of payment fell precipitously, the payment system represented by the circulation of bank deposits was shut down, and credit was curtailed. The collapse of banks led to a steep deflation which caused the wide, deep and protracted output contraction that serve as a definition of a depression. Bound to support the gold standard, the Federal Reserve didn't follow Bagehot's prescription, that is, it didn't serve appropriately as a lender of last resort, so that panic actually degenerated into madness.

Price deflation was an essential link in the downward spiral leading to depression (Fisher, 1932). Falling prices increased the burden of debt for firms at same the time in which it stimulated buyers to refrain from making purchases and wait for even lower prices. Deflation, thus, became a self-feeding process of bankruptcy, more deflation, more bank failures, etc.[2] Characterizing the period, Kindleberger quoted W.A. Lewis to state:

> [t]he essential truth is found in the conventional wisdom that price declines are deflationary in so far as they "check confidence, provoke bank failures, encourage hoarding and in various ways discourage investment."
>
> (Kindleberger 1973: 142)

Inspired by the sequence of events summarily described above, the notion of systemic crisis was born designating a particular event which is amplified until it causes the economy as a whole to be paralyzed. It is the whole system that becomes dysfunctional in such a way that the resumption of normality can only be achieved after a long time and the implementation of wide-ranging reforms, which includes the writing of appropriate financial regulation.

The definition of systemic risk

The stylized description of the great depression offered above has been challenged by many. The most influential alternative explanation, doubtless, was offered by Milton Friedman and Anna Schwartz, suggesting that fateful mistakes committed by the Federal Reserve were actually responsible for transforming the stock exchange crash into a full blown recession in 1931. However, whether Friedman and Schwartz are right or not pertains to the characterization of the trigger of the crisis, not necessarily the characterization of the crisis itself.

In any case, the expression systemic crisis is not used just as a synonym to a standard cyclical recession. The great depression was certainly not a standard recession.[3] Still, depression and systemic crisis are not precisely the same concept either. What does it mean to say that the great depression was a systemic crisis? What makes any crisis a systemic crisis?

There is a variety of definitions of systemic crisis in the literature. In fact, De Bandt and Hartmann (2000) provided a useful survey illustrating how diverse the meanings attributed to the concept may be. Their own choice is a concept according to which

> a systemic crisis (…) can be defined as a systemic event that affects a considerable number of financial institutions and markets in a strong sense [that is, leading to actual bankruptcies in the sector] thereby severely impairing the general functioning (of an important part) of the financial system.
>
> (De Bandt and Hartmann 2000: 11)

Systemic risk, in this context, is the risk of a systemic event taking place which causes a systemic crisis to occur.

De Bandt and Hartmann state that "[a]t the heart of the concept [of systemic risk] is the notion of 'contagion,' a particularly strong propagation of failures from one institution, market or system to another" (De Bandt and Hartmann 2000: 8).[4] However, they note that many authors prefer to define systemic crisis differently, taking it to be the result of a shock wide and strong enough to move an entire *system*, be it the financial system, or the whole economic system, or in fact any other *system*.

The phenomenon of contagion is the object of much dispute. For some, there is not much evidence of its importance. Kaufman and Scott, for instance, state that "[c]ommon-shock systemic risk, particularly in the short-term, appears to be more frequent than chain-reaction systemic risk" (Kaufmann and Scott 2003: 376). In their view, the evidence indicates that problems at one bank or at a group of banks do spill over to other banks in general, but almost exclusively only to banks with the same or similar portfolio-risk exposures and subject to the same shock. There is little if any empirical evidence that the insolvency of an individual bank directly causes the insolvency of economically solvent banks or that bank depositors run on economically solvent banks very often or that, when they do, they drive these banks into insolvency.

(Kaufmann and Scott 2003: 376–377)

They add that

even during the Great Contraction of 1929/1933 and at the height of the banking crisis and bank runs in Chicago in 1932, liquidity problems and depositor runs rarely, if ever, drove economically solvent independent banks into insolvency.

(Kaufmann and Scott 2003: 379)

A second bone of contention relates to the cradle of systemic risk. Goodhart *et al.*, for instance, state that

systemic issues do not relate to all institutions. The key point is that banks are subject to runs, which have contagion effects, and which can throw solvent banks into insolvency both because a large proportion of their assets are not easily marketable and, probably to a lesser extent, because the panic drives down the current value of marketable assets.

(Goodhart *et al.* 1998: 9)

With respect to other segments of financial markets, systemic risk could be irrelevant: "contagion is less likely; and disruption of the payments system does not occur with failure of securities firms" (Goodhart *et al.* 1998: 13). Kaufman and Scott, in contrast, assume that

[s]ystemic risk also may occur in other parts of the financial sector – for example, in securities markets as evidenced by simultaneous declines in the prices of a large number of securities in one or more markets in a single country or across countries.

(Kaufmann and Scott 2003: 372)

This divergence is, on the other hand, related to another, that is the identification of the main channels of contagion of shocks to the real economy. Systemic crises could mean simply that shocks suffered by an institution or a group of financial institutions come to be transmitted to the rest of the financial system. But there is no doubt that the importance that is conferred to systemic risk is because of "the potential of financial shocks to lead to substantial, adverse effects on the economy (…)." (Kambhu *et al.* 2007: 5). As seen in the quotation from Goodhart *et al.* above, a place of honor is reserved in some analyses to the operation of payments systems.[5] They propose that

> there are basically two determinants of systemic stability, the first being the market infrastructure – such as payment systems, clearing houses, etc – which channels the exposures of financial institutions to each other, and the second being individual banks' risk taking within that infrastructure.
>
> (Kambhu *et al.* 2007: 73)

It is precisely because of the role of banks operating one of the main payment systems of a modern economy, which is based on the circulation of demand deposits, that some analysts consider banks as the sole bearer of systemic risks. Herring and Litan, however, suggest that

> securities markets may also generate a contagious spread of losses. A sudden drop in securities prices may prompt further price drops if many market participants are highly leveraged, have purchased their assets on margin, and are forced by the initial price decline to sell their holdings. If, in turn, those who suffer losses cause one or more banks that are central to the payments system to fail, the resulting losses in liquidity may cause credit to contract and the level of real economic activity to fall.
>
> (Herring and Litan 1995: 51)

One should notice, anyway, that Herring and Litan identify a systemic risk in the operation of securities markets through their links with banks. This implicitly suggests that the separation between commercial banks (which accept deposits) and securities markets, Glass–Steagal Act-style could eliminate or significantly attenuate systemic risks coming from securities markets.

But one should also notice that Herring and Litan introduced another link in the transmission belt: credit contraction. In fact, adverse effects on the real economy could also be due to the fall in credit supply that would result from a financial crisis, independently of whether or not the payment system collapsed. However, if it is variations in credit supply that constitute the main channel of contagion of financial crises to the real economy, systemic risk would not be related solely to bank failures.[6]

The obscurities that surround the concept of systemic risk are particularly important because, as argued before, regulation directed at preserving systemic stability is shaped by the diagnosis of systemic risk. One cannot just leave the notion undefined assuming it is somehow obvious.[7] It is not very productive either just to assume operational definitions that cannot be justified on any theoretical basis.[8]

Stability regulation

A regulatory revolution took place in the United States in the 1930s in reaction to the crisis. The main initiatives were inspired by the stylized sequence of events presented above. Rules for protecting the integrity of markets were introduced to curb speculation in the securities markets, and more particularly in the stock exchange. A supervisor was created, the Securities Exchange Commission, to supervise these markets. Its mission was to protect investors. Indirectly, it would help to preserve financial stability because it was believed that a properly supervised market, by protecting investors and keeping them adequately informed about the perspectives for their investments, should avoid panic episodes as the one experienced in 1929. A second crucial step was the breaking up of universal banks imposed by the Glass–Steagall Act. It was expected that banning financial conglomerates controlling both commercial banks and investment banks should severe the connections between securities markets and deposit taking activities, thereby preventing the contagion of a segment's problems to the other. A safety net was created, the main element of which was the introduction of deposit insurance to tranquilize depositors and prevent bank runs. Prudential regulation was imposed on banks to contain their risk exposures and reduce the probability of failure that would activate deposit insurance.

The stability strategy devised in the 1930s turned out to be extremely successful. No serious banking crisis occurred in the United States until the 1980s. In time, however, the very success of stability regulation bred complacency. The events triggering the 1930s crisis were reinterpreted. For some analysts, the result of this reinterpretation was to suggest that the crisis was not due to any structural inadequacy of financial systems but to policy mistakes made by the Federal Reserve. The extended experience with stability led many to take it as proof of the intrinsic systemic stability of financial markets. The debate on regulation, particularly in the United States, shifted focus more and more to market distortions supposedly created by the existence of a safety net. Particularly in the 1980s, one would conclude from a cursory examination of the literature on regulation that the main problem faced by the US banking system was *moral hazard* engendered by the existence of deposit insurance.

Concern with systemic risks and financial crises was characteristic of fringe, non-orthodox schools of economics, like the Post-Keynesian school or some strands of neo-Marxian economics. In the mainstream, one could distinguish three main views, all sharing the basic assessment that financial markets were more stable than was believed in the past. The first view, held by influential economists such as George Kaufman, was that systemic crises were not only extremely rare but, and more importantly, they were not characterized by the deleterious effects that were emphasized in the literature. According to Kaufman, available evidence showed that two of the most deleterious effects didn't really take place. First, contagion didn't hit healthy banks, which was evidence that banking markets were "rational and information-based" (Kaufman and Scott 2003: 380).[9] Second, there was no "empirical evidence that bank failures ever ignited downturns in the macroeconomy" (ibid.). In Kaufman's view, deposit insurance decreased the pressure of market discipline on banks, because now depositors have no incentive to accumulate information on the bank they deal with, and, thus, ironically, contributed to make the banking system more fragile.

The policy implication of these arguments is clear: reduce protection of depositors that market discipline will take the place of regulation, with higher efficiency.

A second view seems to be offered by Goodhart *et al.* (1998). They also seem to assume that financial systems are more stable than is assumed by policy makers, the press, etc. but they insist on the airline principle: airplane accidents are very rare, but when they happen the consequences are so dire that regulation of the activity is necessary to make them even rarer. Thus, Goodhart *et al.* state that the

> probability that the failure of a single bank will induce a systemic problem may be low, but, if systemic failure were to occur, it could be serious and the costs could be high. Thus, regulation to prevent systemic problems may be viewed as an insurance premium against a low-probability occurrence.
>
> (Goodhart *et al.* 1998: 9)

The third view also assumes the fundamental stability of modern financial systems, but emphasize that adverse shocks of exceptional violence may overwhelm the adjustment mechanisms of the economy and put it on a cumulative disequilibria path. An early defender of this view was Irving Fisher. In his famous 1933 article on debt deflation, for instance, he wrote:

> There may be equilibrium which, though stable, is so delicately poised that, after departure from it beyond certain limits, instability ensues, just as, at first, a stick may bend under strain, ready all the time to bend back, until a certain point is reached, when it breaks. This simile probably applies when a debtor gets "broke," or when the breaking of many debtors constitutes a "crash," after which there is no coming back to the original equilibrium.
>
> (Fisher 1933: 339)[10]

As pointed out by Kaufman and Scott,

> to protect against such contingencies, banks employ various risk-management techniques, including the maintenance of higher capital ratios to absorb unexpected losses. It is difficult, however, to anticipate the probability and magnitude of extreme events and hence the amount of capital that an individual bank, given its risk preferences, ought to maintain.
>
> (Kaufman and Scott 2003: 382)

In fact, the maintenance of a given capital ratio as the main pillar of financial stability is the core of the Basel strategy. Another common feature of this strategy is the reliance on market-friendly rules, which rely on *best practices* of risk management adopted by banks and other financial institutions to control systemic risk.[11] One can doubt, however, the adequacy of this approach if one remembers that financial stability is a public good, anyway, a positive externality that, as such, will never be properly guaranteed only (or even mainly) by private means. As a matter of fact, the current financial crisis is evidence of the widespread failure of private risk management techniques to prevent a large scale financial disaster.

3 Systemic crisis: a post Keynesian perspective

The Post Keynesian starting point for the analysis of systemic risk and systemic crisis, as well as the analysis of stability regulation, is, of course, Keynes's liquidity preference theory and Hyman Minsky's elaboration of liquidity preference in his Financial Instability Hypothesis (FIH). Minsky once summarized FIH as a set of two *theorems*:

> The first theorem of the financial instability hypothesis is that the economy has financing regimes under which it is stable and financing regimes under which it is unstable. The second theorem is that, over periods of prolonged prosperity, the economy moves from financial relations that make for a stable system to those that make for an unstable system.
>
> (Minsky 1994: 157)

The aphorism Minsky himself created to encapsulate his theory is well-known: *stability is destabilizing*. In fact, the aphorism nicely presents the main point of contrast between the Post Keynesian and the orthodox perspectives on systemic risk: while the latter presumes a financial system that is intrinsically stable, except for major adverse shocks, the former takes instability generation as a normal feature of the workings of the financial system. In other words, while orthodox economists believe that at least the probability is very high that financial markets tend to reach and remain spontaneously in durable, stable equilibrium positions, Minsky's FIH states that even if equilibrium positions are eventually reached, they will not last, because there are endogenous forces pushing to undo them. As a consequence, the typical stylization of systemic crisis offered by orthodox economists is that of a naturally stable system being hit by exceptionally strong shocks, *extreme events* as put by Kaufman and Scott. Post Keynesians, in contrast, offer an alternative stylization, that of a system that continually builds disequilibria and becomes progressively more fragile until the point where even a small shock can generate a major crisis. Besides, once this happens, the same mechanisms that led to growing disequilibria respond for the tendency of the "real" economy to rapidly shrink.

The key to the Post Keynesian approach is to understand leverage. Operating with borrowed money, under normal conditions, which means that when rates of interest on loans are lower than rates of return on the investment made with the borrowed money, is a powerful way to augment profits.[12] Leverage extends the reach of enterprise, but it also extends the reach of speculation. Of course, neither lenders nor borrowers can escape the fundamental uncertainty that surrounds the future. Therefore, borrowers and, still more obviously, lenders, must take precautions to try to keep the risks they are exposed to under control. These precautions are the margins of safety a lender establishes when allowing a borrower to increase his leverage:

> A fundamental property of all capitalist economies is the existence of a system of borrowing and lending based upon various margins of safety. The excess of anticipated cash flows from asset ownership or participation in income production over the cash flows committed by the liability structure is one class of margins of safety. The excess of the market or the pledge value of assets over the value of liabilities which can require the payment of some principle amount is another class of margins of safety.
>
> (Minsky 1991: 12)[13]

The behavior of margins of safety is an essential element of Minsky's approach to financial crises. At any given point in time, the size of margins at the same time informs the confidence economic agents have in their future prospects, the limits that are being imposed on the extent of new loan commitments (and on the investments that may be financed by them) and the cushion protecting lenders in case of disappointment of expectations. Keeping margins of safety, thus, means missing gain opportunities in exchange for a fall back if things go wrong. If things do go right, on the other hand, both borrowers and lenders may feel that they lost an opportunity to increase their gains because they overestimated the risks to which they were exposed.

The size of margins changes when estimates of probabilities of repayment of the loan change. This may happen when the experience of stability lasts long enough to convince people that prosperity is permanent and that whatever threats were suffered in the past are not likely to be repeated. The state of confidence is strengthened and more optimistic expectations about the future are held allowing for an expansion of enterprise based on increasing leverage and decreasing margins of safety.[14] Keynes in fact discussed the possibility of favorable current results influencing positively the expectations of entrepreneurs, stating that

> as regards psychology, I maintain that if I am right that a large capital programme would increase the profits of businessmen, this would, after the first blush, have more effect on them than anything else. (...). In the long run we do not see how business confidence is likely to be maintained otherwise than by an actual recovery of business profits.
>
> (CW 20: 361, 444)[15]

More recently, margins have tended to change also in a more mechanistic way. The widespread use of statistical models to manage risk has increased the use of statistical series to quantify probabilities of default and other risks. Long-lasting periods of stability tend to feed into these models leading to a reduction in calculated loss probabilities and to increasing levels of leverage, automatically reducing margins of safety. The reliance on these models, as has become clear in the current crisis, strengthened the feedback effects through which leverage tends to increase monotonically.[16]

Leverage, thus, grows during prosperity phases, intensifying and accelerating growth and prosperity itself.[17] However, increasing leverage means also increasing fragility. With lower and lower margins of safety, lenders become more and more exposed to shocks that could be small and fundamentally harmless under ordinary circumstances, as Keynes argued.

But dangerous as rising leverage is in itself, it also makes room for a more immediate threat: illiquidity. When borrowing to buy assets, the investor is faced with the choice of the maturity he or she desires for the loans that may be needed. As illustrated by the normal shape of yield curves, shorter-maturity loans usually charge lower interest rates than longer-maturity loans. The difference between them obviously tempts borrowers to borrow short-term loans to buy longer term assets, in order to pocket the interest rate spread between them. Exploring yield curve differences in interest rate, however, exposes the asset buyer to liquidity risks, in this case the risk being of find oneself unable to honor one's liabilities when they come due coupled with the risk of being unable to roll over those debts. Leverage itself exposes the asset holder to insolvency risk, but maturity mismatches between assets and liabilities expose him or her to illiquidity risk. In fact, illiquidity may force the asset holder to fire sale his assets to pay his or her debts, forcing their prices down and making him or her insolvent, even if in the absence of the fire sale the present value of assets was higher than that of liabilities.

As it is well known, Minsky defined three financial postures, corresponding to different degrees of fragility. Hedge financing is the safest posture, maintaining a wide margin of safety in the form of the spread between expected returns from assets and committed cash outflows on liabilities while avoiding any maturity mismatch between assets and liabilities. Speculative financing involves the eventual need to roll over principal and Ponzi financing requires lenders to be willing to capitalize due interest, in addition to rolling over principal, resulting in increasing values for debt. Minsky presents his increasing fragility thesis as follows:

> A fundamental conjecture of a model of the economy that supports the Keynes view is that when hedge financing is the dominant posture the interest rate structure offers inducements to increase indebtedness and increase the proportion of short term financing that requires the rolling over of outstanding debts. Once there is a large volume of short term debts outstanding, which finance longer term positions, and institutions exist where such short term debts are regularly rolled over, then a rise in interest rates, a shortfall of earnings or an optimism about future cash flows can lead to the emergence of Ponzi financing relations.
>
> (Minsky 1991: 15)

When speculative and Ponzi borrowers are dominant in the universe of asset-holders, the economy is exposed to systemic risk, because even a small disappointment, like a small rise in interest rates or the deceleration of the growth in the supply of credit, or a disappointment in profit expectations can lead to a massive de-leveraging process. The central point though is that increasing fragility is a natural result of the way the system operates: "The fundamental assertion of the financial instability hypothesis is that the financial structure evolves from being robust to being fragile over a period in which the economy does well" (Minsky 1991: 16).

If new credit cannot be achieved, speculative and Ponzi borrowers are forced to liquidate their assets to settle their debts, selling position to make position, in Minsky's words. Fire sales of assets lead to what Fisher (1933) called debt deflation, a process that Minsky incorporates into his own approach.[18] Debt deflation is an important process in the downward stage of the cycle both because it engenders a cumulative reduction of asset prices that may end up destroying a significant share of the financial wealth of a community and because it serves as a contagion mechanism. When assets are devalued because of fire sales, other individuals and institutions that may hold them in their portfolio also suffer the effects of the devaluation and may eventually become insolvent if the market value of the said assets falls below a certain threshold.

It is important to notice that systemic risk in Minsky's approach is not exclusively or even mainly attributable to characteristics of modern banking systems. In fact, as suggested by Kregel (2008), systemic risk can equally be generated by securities markets, or through the connections between banking and securities markets. The traditional stress on payment systems is actually absent from Minsky's model. Contagion is also less relevant, although, as we have just indicated, it is an important feature of debt deflation processes. Finally, the size of shocks is also irrelevant. One is not dealing with fundamentally stable systems that have to suffer a extremely violent impact to be taken away from equilibrium, as it is the dominant view in the orthodox schools of thought. Instead of the systemic events that are at the core of the conventional concept of systemic crisis, according to De Bandt and Hartmann, Post Keynesians emphasize the continuously operating processes that make financial systems more and more fragile, to the point of being eventually unable to absorb even relatively small shocks. As Galbraith put it, "it is in the nature of a speculative boom that almost anything can collapse it" (Galbraith 1997: 90). What Minsky basically showed is that speculative booms are always being engendered when prolonged stability is experienced.

4 Concluding remarks: post Keynesian perspectives on systemic stability regulation

There is a consensus presently that the current financial crisis is the result of a massive regulatory failure. There is no consensus, however, as to the nature of this failure.

As should be clear from the preceding discussion, preventing systemic crises, from a Post Keynesian point of view, does not require preparing against major surprising adverse shocks, but, rather, preventing fragility from becoming so acute that even a minor shock could derail the operation of the financial system, cause a debt deflation and lead to economic contraction. Successful stability regulation, therefore, must pay attention to the evolution of financial fragility instead of drawing hypothetical defenses against an all-out attack.

The evidence from current crisis so far seems to confirm the Post-Keynesian view. There was no large shock impacting the financial system. The trigger of the crisis seems to have been the resetting of interest rates prescribed in adjustable-rate sub-prime mortgages which led to a reassessment of credit risks.[19] What followed seems to be explainable mostly by the context of extremely highly leveraged financial institutions and of highly leveraged financial markets in general, where layers and layers of new debt securities were created on the basis of the original mortgage contracts and other underlying assets. In Minsky's terms, margins of safety had been reduced to extremely low sizes, eliminating any possibility of preventing the increase in non-performing credits or other such event from having significant impacts on balance sheets of financial institutions.

Therefore, the first pillar of a Post Keynesian strategy of systemic stability regulation is to control leverage and maturity mismatches between assets and liabilities, and preserve margins of safety. Second, stability regulation cannot be confined to banks. Securities markets, at least nowadays, after the spread of securitization, with the heavy involvement of the banking sector in securities markets, became an important link in the debt deflation process. Systemic stability requires, thus, that either the issuance of debt securities are monitored for the systemic risks it may create or that securitization is at least partly rolled back.[20]

A third pillar of Post Keynesian financial regulation is to roll back the privatization of systemic stability regulation that was initiated simultaneously with the de-regulation movement in the 1980s. It is not only that the evaluation of potentially systemic risks cannot be left to entities such as rating agencies, with all their conflicts of interest. The attempt to use banks' *best practices* as instruments of systemic risk control, which was a core element of Basel II, didn't work well either. Models for measurement of risk such as the VaR (value-at-risk) models promoted by the Basel Committee worked to amplify or to disguise risks instead of controlling them. But beyond the inadequacies of a particular statistical model, or family of models, the fact remains that systemic stability is a public good, that will not be *produced* in optimal quantities by private decision. At least in part, Basel III is evidence that even the Basel Committee has finally realized it.

A fourth pillar is that, for the reasons just given, market discipline will always play, at best, a subordinated role in the attempt to guarantee systemic stability. It is a heroic assumption to suggest that customers of financial services could actually judge risk exposures in the various financial institutions and markets. Well-informed market participants, like money market or pension fund managers, on the other hand, frequently maintain too complex relations among themselves and with financial institutions to be trusted with the mission of preserving financial stability. Finally, in the Post Keynesian approach, markets cannot control risk exposure, financial fragility and reduction of margins of safety because both borrowers and lenders are affected by the same general business atmosphere that underlie all risk evaluations.

A last pillar results from Minsky's theory of financial innovation, not discussed in this chapter.[21] Financial institutions continuously implement and develop financial innovations to increase their profits. Many of these innovations, in fact, are attempts to circumvent regulations that prevent them from excessively exposing themselves to risk or to increase leverage beyond what is considered safe or reasonable. Neoliberal critics of financial regulations sometimes raise the argument that it is useless to try to regulate financial markets because innovation will always defeat it.[22] The Post Keynesian approach fully recognizes this possibility and that financial institutions will insistently try to defeat any regulation that reduces their perceived profit opportunities. As Minsky noted,

> the Keynesian view recognizes that agents learn and adapt, so that a system of intervention that was apt under one set of circumstances can become inept as the economy evolves.
>
> (Minsky 1991: 7)

Nevertheless, this is not a valid argument against regulation, although it is a warning that no specific system of rules is ever optimal regardless of circumstances.

These five pillars embody the fundamental Post-Keynesian perspective that it is increasing fragility that should be targeted by systemic stability regulation, because the reduction of margins of safety are inherent to capitalist dynamics, instead of the prevention against *one-in-a-hundred-years* events that escaped detection by risk management systems of private financial institutions operating in intrinsically stable markets.

Notes

1 See, for example, Temin (1976), Friedman and Schwartz (1963) and Bernanke (2000).
2 Keynes had also warned about this possibility. Explaining why the elasticity of substitution of money is zero

> or nearly equal, to zero; which means that as the exchange value of money rises there is no tendency to substitute some other factor for it (...). This follows from the peculiarity of money that its utility is solely derived from its exchange-value, so that the two rise and fall pari passu, with the result that as the exchange value of money rises there is no motive or tendency, as in the case of rent-factors, to substitute some other factor for it. Thus, not only is it impossible to turn more labour on to producing money when its labour-price rises, but money is a bottomless sink for purchasing power, when the demand for it increases, since there is no value for it at which demand is diverted – as in the case of other rent-factors – so as to slop over into a demand for other things.
>
> (CW 7: 231)

3 Schumpeter (2005: 145–155) discusses the extent to which recession and depression may be seen as different phenomena. A recession, according to Schumpeter, is a normal stage in the evolution of a capitalist economy, a stage in its process of adaptation to the introduction of major innovations. A depression, said Schumpeter, is pathological, an exceptional development, with distinct properties, in which downward spirals emerge to take the economy to bottom of the pit and keep it there.

4 Herring and Litan (1995: 50) also define systemic risk as "the possibility of a contagious spread of losses across financial institutions that threatens to harm the real economy (the production of goods and services)."

5

> Payments and settlement systems are potentially a key institutional channel for the propagation of systemic crises. The failure of one or more institutions to settle or the fear that they might be unable to do so can trigger and spread a financial disturbance. And disruptions to the payment system can have repercussions throughout the economy: all economic activity is predicated on the ability to settle transactions and confidence that counterparties will do likewise.
>
> BIS (1994: 177)

6 As Kambhu *et al.* (2007: 6) put it: "(...) these real effects might occur if credit provision is interrupted through shocks to the banking sector or through capital market disruptions."

7 Federal Reserve Board Vice-Chairman Donald Kohn, for instance, gave a speech on the theme *Risk management and its implications for systemic risk*, where the expression *systemic risk* is actually not referred even once, let alone rigorously defined! Cf. Kohn (2008).

8 Cf. Barth *et al.* (2006), in an otherwise very interesting work, where systemic crises are defined by a purely quantitative criterion. Drawing on a list of bank distress experiences, they classify an episode as

> systemic if emergency measures were taken to assist the banking system (such as banking holidays, deposit freezes, blanket guarantees to depositors or other bank creditors), or if large-scale nationalizations took place. Episodes were also classified as systemic if nonperforming assets reached at least 10 percent of total assets at the peak of the crisis, or if the cost of the rescue operations was at least 2 percent of GDP.
>
> (Barth *et al.* 2006: 213)

The authors concede that "there is an inherent arbitrariness in distinguishing a 'systemic' crisis from a 'large' crisis, of from a situation where a well-known banks fails" (ibid.). In their view, a systemic crisis does not involve any particular dynamic. Systemic merely means large.

9 Some of this evidence has been disputed by Richardson (2006), who shows that Federal Reserve data suggest that a variety of bank distress episodes actually took place in the period, defying simple generalizations.

10 A non-orthodox similar view is offered in the form of the *corridor concept*. Cf. Leijonhufvud (1981), Chapter 6. As will be seen in the next section, Minsky relied heavily on Fisher's paper and made the concept of debt deflation a central part of his own approach. However, the main difference between the two authors is that Minsky does not assume a stable financial system but, on the contrary, an endogenously ever-destabilizing financial system, where debt deflation is one of the processes that define instability.

11 Even Goodhart *et al.*, who recognize that systemic threats, even if rare, can be exceedingly dangerous, propose that "less emphasis should be placed on detailed and prescriptive rules and more on internal risk analysis, management and control systems.

(...). More reliance needs to be placed on institutions' own internal risk analysis, management and control systems." (Goodhart *et al.* 1998: 194) They do remind us that "this does not imply that there is no role for rules. It is not a question of internal v. external regulation: both must be involved." (ibid.). This is not, however, the way stability regulation has evolved and Basel II would take the system even further in the direction of the *privatisation* of stability regulation. After the 2007 crisis began, however, Goodhart, if not necessarily his co-authors, seems to have changed his views. See Goodhart (2009). The Basel Committee itself, in fact, seemed to have second thoughts about its strategy after the crisis began and made the shortcomings of Basel II impossible to ignore. Basel III, which has since been launched in reaction to the crisis, incorporates some of the concerns identified below, in Section 3. See Cardim de Carvalho (forthcoming).

12 In fact, few authors illustrated this argument so cogently as Bagehot (1994: 4).

13 As Keynes argued, these margins serve as cushion to absorb deviations from expected results of a deal when a bank lends money to a borrower:

> For the banks allow beforehand for some measure of fluctuation in the value both of particular assets and of real assets in general, by requiring from the borrower what is conveniently called a "margin." That is to say, they will only lend him money up to a certain proportion of the value of the asset which is the "security" offered by the borrower to the lender. Experience has led to the fixing of conventional percentages for the "margin" as being reasonably safe in all *ordinary* circumstances.
>
> (Keynes 1963: 170–171, my emphasis)

14 Joan Robinson (1979), recognized that "borrowers must provide lenders with more than their own hopes, and investment plans are limited by the supply of finance." However, uncertainty depends on the state of confidence. "Thus, the supply of finance cannot be regarded as a rigid bottleneck limiting the rate of investment, but must be treated rather as an element in the general atmosphere encouraging or retarding accumulation." (Robinson 1979: 14–21) This is the *subjective* aspect, which was emphasized by Minsky.

15 The acknowledgement of the disproportional influence of short-term memory on economic decision-making has been one of the pillars of behavioral finance.

16 An excellent paper by Jan Kregel (2008) stresses precisely the automatization of credit concession brought about by securitization, in contrast to the credit decision by banks, based on individualized information about the borrower, as one of the central characteristics of the present crisis and one of the aspects of Minsky's original model in need of modernization.

17 Galbraith (1997) lays on the purchase of stocks on margin the main blame both for the unbridled speculation of the late 1920s and the crash of 1929. See also Kindleberger (1973: 118–119).

18 Minsky actually modifies Fisher's original debt deflation concept making it relate to the price of assets instead of goods, as in Fisher's original formulation (Fisher, 1932).

19 Others point to changes in the prices of houses. See Chapter 9, below.

20 Minsky in fact defended the Glass–Steagall Act against the critics that defended the adoption of the universal banking model in the United States.

21 For a discussion of Minsky's theory of financial innovation, see Minsky (1982), Chapter 7.

22 The same point is also raised with respect to capital controls.

Part IV
Macroeconomic policy

8 Economic policies for monetary economies

1 Introduction

Entrepreneurial economies allow individuals to accumulate wealth in monetary form when they feel insecure about the opportunities to commit themselves to more profitable alternatives. Wealth holders seek to protect their capital by accumulating highly liquid assets when the confidence they have in their own expectations is low. The problem, however, is that when individuals direct their asset demand toward liquid assets, they accumulate irreproducible assets, the creation of which did not absorb any labor. Therefore, all else remaining the same, when liquidity preference rises, output and employment fall. Private individuals and firms cannot be relied upon, in these circumstances, to support the level of aggregate demand which would avoid the fall. This is the fundamental challenge the existence of liquidity preference poses for government macroeconomic policy makers in an entrepreneurial economy.

The problem, as Keynes described in the GT, is *systemic*, that is, it is rooted in the way the economic system is structured. Production and capital accumulation is performed mostly by private firms and people, who coordinate their activities through a system of money contracts. Keynes argued that this is a very efficacious way to organize economic activity, that has been proved far superior to the alternatives that were tried during the twentieth-century in the form of command economies (like fascist and communist regimes, most of which crumbled under the weight of their own inadequacies). But the same system of money contracts which supports the entrepreneurial organization of production is what makes money so attractive an asset that it can take the place of capital goods in the "portfolios" of investors. When it does, as already pointed out, output and employment fall and can remain down for extended periods of time, if nothing is done to change the situation. In the Keynesian view, there is no way to eliminate the dilemma: the same properties that make modern economies so dynamic are the ones responding for their inability to sustain full employment.

There can be no doubt that, personally, Keynes was a strong believer in the state's ability to positively intervene in the economy. The policy implications of the GT are clear: entrepreneurial economies cannot maintain, spontaneously, full employment and full utilization of available productive capacity. From time to time, the machine will break down and grind to a halt. Differently from business cycle theorists who also recognized that modern economies periodically experience falls in output and employment but believed that the economy would automatically mend its ways, Keynes believed that, beyond any possible cyclical dynamics, entrepreneurial economies could also face durable disequilibria, in fact so durable that they could be seen as new equilibria, characterized by high rates of unemployment. It was with these latter problems that Keynes was worried. It was to break unsatisfactory states of the economy that could last a long time, even if not forever, that government policies had to be devised.

From the reading of the GT, however, it is still obscure what kind of policies Keynes in fact defended. Most of the time, what is taken to be "Keynesian policies" come from Keynes's texts written much before the GT or from authors that freely interpret not only what was the "true" core of the GT and what policies should follow from it. Very little attention was given to Keynes's actual proposals made *after* the publication of the GT, when, arguably, he had a clearer view of the nature of problems faced by an entrepreneurial economy. A particularly rich material that has not received the attention it deserves consist in the proposals made during the war and for the post war period. These proposals occupy in fact a few volumes of his Collected Writings and will be extensively used in the discussion that follows.[1]

2 The need for intervention

In the final chapter of the GT, Keynes identified the two major evils of modern capitalism as being an excessive degree of income concentration and the system's inability to sustain the full employment of its workers and productive capacity. Keynes considered the latter problem the worst of the two, since ways could be devised to attenuate income and wealth inequalities. Keynes, like Schumpeter, did not consider complete equality a valid goal because different rewards should accrue to people on account of their differences in willingness to work, efficiency, aversion to risk, etc. The problem was not that income was not equally distributed but that it was concentrated beyond the point in which it is justified by those reasons. Excessive income and wealth concentration were serious problems of modern economies, threatening the cohesion of societies and the stability of democratic rules. Keynes considered them, however, of comparatively easy solution. While, as argued above, entrepreneurial economies do engender some social differentiation and inequality, excessive inequality was generated by mechanisms that were not intrinsic to this type of social organization. One of the targets of Keynes's constant criticism was the right of inheritance. Inequality generated by differences in talent or in effort was necessary to stimulate enterprise. Inequality due to inheritance rewards nothing, it only gives starting advantages to some individuals, that have nothing to do with their eventual contribution to society, and therefore does not touch the incentive structure that has supported the efficacy of this type of economic organization.

Being extrinsic to the system, excess concentration could be corrected, for example, through the imposition of progressive income and wealth taxes and taxes on inheritance, and the provision of public goods.

As to the inability to sustain continuously full employment, the problem, as mentioned above, is different. Effective Demand could be too low, with respect to productive potential, because uncertainty is pervasive and private agents frequently try to avoid it by taking refuge in the accumulation of liquid assets. The problem is more complex than the distribution question. Uncertainty cannot be eliminated and the institutions created to reduce its burden enough to allow the economy to work, among which the creation of a system of forward money contracts may be the most important, are also the causes of deficient demand, as was extensively discussed in this book. One cannot "correct" the rules of the economic system to eliminate the possibility of deficient aggregate demand. "Outside" intervention may be required.[2] The State is the obvious, or, in fact, the only, candidate to perform this intervention.

Keynes was careful to point out that effective demand problems were not caused by relative price imbalances, by market imperfections or by difficulties to allocate currently produced goods. He accepted the Marshallian view that allocation of goods and services throughout the economy was to be ultimately decided by private agents receiving price signals from markets. Elimination of private property to transfer allocative decisions to the State was explicitly rejected by Keynes (CW 7: 378). The flaw in the system had to do with the *volume* of expenditure, not its composition. It was not to be sought in relative prices of goods, but of assets. Because of uncertainty, prices of assets were set in a way that penalized capital goods, because of its higher illiquidity. Low or null liquidity premia frequently caused prices of capital assets to fall below their flow supply prices, depressing investment, which, through the multiplier, led to a fall in consumption, and therefore of aggregate demand.

The only way left to escape this fix, in the Keynesian approach, is to create new sources of aggregate demand, outside the private sector, to be added to private consumption and private investment demand. The liquidity preference approach to Keynesian theory postulates the need for such form of intervention if full employment is to be preserved.

3 The possibility of intervention

Just to spot a systemic flaw, no matter how important the flaw may be, is not enough, in itself, to justify state intervention. To call for government action it is also necessary, and it is important to note that this is an *independent* assumption, to suppose that the state is *capable* of dealing with the problem, which is by no means self evident. The point raised by critics of government actions, that policy failures may be worse than market failures, should be taken seriously, since there are plenty of examples of misdesigned policies aggravating problems rather than solving them even in recent experience. In other words, to point out that private agents are not capable by themselves of ensuring continuous full employment does not *imply* that the state could do better. The solution may very well be beyond the possibility of conscious intervention.

This was, in fact, the view of most of business cycle theorists, that used to assume that recessions were the necessary consequence of prosperity. Some even took the argument to the point of suggesting that crises acted as cleansing mechanisms in the economy, allowing it to get rid of less productive producers and releasing factors of production to better use in the surviving firms. Recessions eventually dissipate and cede place to recoveries, just to reappear in the future, and nothing could or should be done about it. To stop recessions allows non-competitive firms to survive and perpetuates inefficient uses of available production factors. Government intervention distorts incentives to innovate and to improve production methods, the choices of workers between labor and leisure and condemns economies to mediocre results, not to speak of accessory problems, like stimulating corruption, cronyism, rent-seeking behavior, etc.

Keynes, however, disagreed with most or all of these arguments. He did not see the point of inflicting losses on firms and workers for reasons that were actually beyond their control, being *macroeconomic* in origin. Fluctuations in confidence and the perception of uncertainty could lead to a fall of aggregate demand that would kill even efficient producers. Supporting aggregate demand does not eliminate competition among firms, as it is not reasonable to propose that more competitive firms would be content with merely keeping their market share instead of extending it. In any case, forcing bankruptcies and unemployment is a wasteful method of "adjusting" the economy. For Keynes, and most of his followers, it is an obligation of economists to search for better methods of improving the quality of production methods.

At the time Keynes wrote the GT, the strongest criticism of government intervention was not directed against aggregate demand management, which was not practiced anywhere as such. The controversy then centered on the possibility of governments replacing markets as allocation mechanisms, in the context of the debate around the viability of socialist, or command, economies. This debate was *not* motivated by the Russian revolution of 1917, it, in fact, originated in works published in the last years of the nineteenth century. A socialist economy was conceived as one in which allocation of factors of production and finished goods would be made by other methods than the markets utilized in capitalist economies. The debate, accordingly, centered on the question of whether the state could collect the necessary information to orient efficiently its production decisions. The debate lasted decades, with most participants arguing that, although it was theoretically conceivable that the state could collect all the necessary information from engineers (about production methods), consumers (about preferences), workers (about qualifications, willingness to work, among other determinants of the availability and quality of labor), and so on, in practice it was inconceivable that an actual government could gather and process the information within acceptable periods of time. Participants of this debate, such as Hayek, argued that the superiority of markets resided precisely in the decentralized nature of decision making they entailed.[3]

The controversy about the viability of non-market economies, thus, dealt with the possibility of substituting central planning for the price mechanism. Keynes posed an entirely different problem: is it possible to sustain capital asset prices in the face of contractionary pressures in order to avoid a retrenchment of investment which could lead to a deficiency of aggregate demand?

The problem, as postulated by Keynes, is much less complex than that posed by defenders of central planning. It is not allocation that matters, but global utilization of productive capacity (inclusive of labor). Maladjustments to be corrected do not need to be sought in relative prices of an impossibly large number of goods, but in the comparison of basically two variables: aggregate value of demand and the value of full employment output. Moreover, the solution consists in increasing (or decreasing, as the case may be) total demand to adjust it to full employment output.

In fact, the Gordian knot was cut even further. One can conceive at least three possible kinds of policy instruments to solve the Keynesian problem:

1   the state could assume direct responsibility for investment decisions;
2   the state could try to offer incentives to private investments in selected areas; and
3   the state could seek to affect overall private investment by creating a safer economic environment within which private investors could feel stimulated to make riskier bets than merely accumulating liquid assets.

The first policy, that some take to be the meaning of Keynes's somewhat cryptic reference to a desirable "socialization of investment" (CW 7: 378), goes at least in part against the intent to preserve private decision-making and should be ruled out as a *general* strategy, even if expanding public investment in *certain areas* could be desirable. As Keynes put it, the point was to make free enterprise work, not to kill it.[4] The second line of policy would involve the state directly in the process of resource allocation, something that in principle nor only could require more information than governments usually have at their disposal, but also make governments to distribute favors in unequal proportions among their constituents, which poses a different sort of political problems. In any case, at least Keynes himself personally favored some types of industrial policy, although it does not result necessarily from the theory of entrepreneurial economies.[5]

It was the third kind of policy that was preferred by Keynes. In a series of articles published in *The Times* in early 1937, Keynes recognized the difficulty of substituting government planning of investments for private accumulation decisions. The main role of government should not be to take the place of private markets. Intervention should be designed to boost aggregate demand thereby reducing overall uncertainty as to the prospects for the whole economy.

The ideal macroeconomic policy proposed by Keynes would be to inflate aggregate demand, expanding the economy like pumping air into a balloon, leaving to private agents the decisions as to how the resources would be employed. In short, the effective demand problem is that capital asset values are depressed by income uncertainty and illiquidity. Boosting aggregate demand reduces both. Thus, it should raise demand prices of that kind of assets. A rising tide would not lift all boats, but it was mainly to private agents to decide which boats should float and which ones should sink.[6] To do it, the government should implement investments of their own, in projects that would not compete with private investment, creating thereby an environment favorable to private initiative. The *pace* of investments would be regulated according to the need to compensate private demand deficiencies to sustain a stable level of aggregate demand over time corresponding to full employment.

Keynes was a firm believer in the possibility that an enlightened government could implement such policies. He also believed that the GT had finally laid the foundations for the development of scientific macroeconomic management. A few years earlier, Keynes had welcomed the creation of an economic advisory body to the Prime Minister with these words:

> ... a move along these lines would indeed be an act of statesmanship, the importance of which cannot easily be exaggerated. For it would mark a transition in our conceptions of the functions and purposes of the state, and a first measure towards the deliberate and purposive guidance of the evolution of our economic life. It would be a recognition of the enormous part to be applied in this by the scientific spirit as distinct from the sterility of the purely party attitude ...
>
> (CW 20: 27)

The possibility of planning, in the sense of preparing intervention plans to compensate for the eventual lack of private investments, was enhanced, in Keynes's view, by the fact that government is not just another guess-maker as to future trends, but it is, to a large extent, a builder of the future, through its power to mobilize resources and to move aggregate demand.[7] Its sphere of action should not overlap with the private sphere. On the contrary, government should help to create a stable and safe environment for private agents to act. It was for this reason that Keynes could write to Hayek, after receiving a copy of the latter's newly published liberal pamphlet *The Road to Serfdom*, that he sympathized with Hayek's moral stand but believed that more, not less, planning was necessary to guarantee the freedom of men (CW 27: 385–388). These political concerns, besides considerations of efficiency, also led Keynes to propose, in his *Essays in Persuasion*, that public investments should be implemented by *semiautonomous public bodies*, entities that were not private but were not part of government either.

In sum, Keynes believed in *the need and the possibility* of government intervention to guarantee full employment. The generally held impression that Keynes favored government's economic activism is correct. The appropriate means to intervene, however, proposed by Keynes were quite different from what was known at his time and turn out to be quite different from what most people, after World War II, judged to be Keynesian policies.

4 The patterns of intervention

An implication of the preceding argument is that the particular character of Keynes's policy proposals consists in the definition of a set of measures designed to reduce or socialize the uncertainties that surround economic decisions and to boost aggregate demand through state intervention when private demand fails. That is the main way in which the state could contribute to create a stable environment for private investors, where entrepreneurs could feel that they would not be hit by fluctuations of aggregate demand beyond their control. Government cannot (and should not) create stable *microeconomic* contexts. Private agents must still face the specific risks surrounding their investment decisions to be able to profit from their eventual successes. But government can reduce or eliminate *macroeconomic* risks, those that affect the economy as a whole and that may punish even those individuals whose decisions are adequate or efficient in microeconomic terms. That is the fundamental perspective orienting Keynes's policies.

Government has at its disposal an arsenal of measures to act upon the overall level of activity. The information to do it is or can be easily generated. As uncertainty is pervasive and flow through many channels, all levers must be pulled to ensure that the economy will move along a path of prosperity. Keynesian policies must consist of *concerted* actions in a multiplicity of arenas.

The need for comprehensive and concerted action is an aspect of Keynes's policy proposals that goes often unnoticed. Uncertainty can affect the economy in many ways. Consumers may fear for their incomes, their jobs, the prices of goods and services they buy, their availability, etc. Entrepreneurs may have to face technological innovations, creations of new goods, changes in tastes, changes in the availability (and costs) of factors of production, changes in the access to markets, etc. Of course, uncertainties can be generated by the state intervention itself: economies where aggregate demand is permanently sustained at high levels may become inflation-prone, higher state expenditures may lead to higher taxes or to higher interest rates if suitable monetary policies are not implemented, competitive advantages may be distributed asymmetrically as a result of public spending, etc. Isolated stimulus policies can end up exerting pressures on other areas of the economy. Uncertainty-reducing intervention requires concerted action in many fronts to avoid that local or sectoral policies end up just deviating uncertainty from its original points of impact instead of the intended reduction.

Therefore, it is better to speak of *Keynesian policies* or, perhaps better since it emphasizes the need for coordination of several policies, *Keynesian strategies* instead of a Keynesian *fiscal* policy or a Keynesian *monetary* policy. Moreover, one must also remember that the "real" nature of "monetary" variables is an essential pillar of Keynes's theory of an entrepreneur economy. Objectives cannot be pursued for a "side" of the economy, neglecting what is happening with the other . Specific recommendations are made for each set of instruments, but it is the integrated nature of macroeconomic management that is the central characteristic of Keynesian policies. The choice of instruments within each set of policies obeys its own logic. Each policy instrument impacts the economy in a specific point of impact, spreads out through specific channels, with its own timing and speed. Moreover, some instruments are easier to control and manipulate than others or are more predictable in the behaviors they induce than others. A comprehensive strategy must be devised in order to use each tool to its maximum efficiency.

Purely macroeconomic policies, in any case, can hardly be conceived. There are no instruments that are able to impact the economy as a whole without changing in some degree its structure, that is, without favoring (or penalizing) some sectors over others. The *art* of economic policy, as it used to be said, must reside precisely in the ability to devise policies for which such effects are either minimized, compensated by other policies, or, if it be the case, be consciously sought, as it may happen when sectoral bottlenecks emerge or depressed areas are targeted for uplifting.

Fiscal Policy[8]

Activist fiscal policy, that is, the conscious appeal to the state's taxing and spending powers to influence aggregate demand, is the best known instrument of Keynesian policy. One needs not to subscribe to the fiscalist approach typical of the neo-classical synthesis Keynesians to realize that the main responsibility for maintaining macroeconomic stability is in effect to be borne by fiscal policy. As we will see below, Keynes did not doubt the efficacy of monetary policy, except under extreme conditions, but he did question the wisdom of relying on interest rate changes as the sole, or even the main, tool for stabilizing income.

Fiscal policy became a very powerful lever to push aggregate demand up or down for two reasons. First, because the share of the state in GDP has grown significantly after World War II, so that its decisions cannot but have a large impact on the level of activity. Second, because it impacts private agents ability to spend: fiscal policy increases or decreases income for those who supply goods and services to the government as well as those who pay taxes. Government taxing and spending trigger a multiplier effect on consumption expenditures just as much as private investment. In particular, spending policies should have a direct impact on the aggregate demand for real capital assets (if private expectations are not affected adversely, which should not happen except under exceptional circumstances):

1   on the one hand, they raise capital asset demand prices, since higher aggregate demand improves the profitability for all investors;
2   they also act through improving the liquidity position of those who have debts outstanding, a kind of *Minsky effect*.

To implement an activist fiscal policy along the lines proposed by Keynes, the government should prepare two fiscal budgets. The first would deal with the ordinary functions of public administration, the *current budget*. The second would focus on government's discretionary spending, the *capital budget*. The current budget, Keynes recommended, should be balanced at all times (CW 27: 225). There should be routine sources of finance for these expenditures to ensure that, in times of prosperity, when aggregate demand was already high, the performance of the normal functions of government would not create any inflationary pressure on the economy. The current budget was to be calculated without direct concern with stabilization needs. The capital budget, dealing with public discretionary spending, was the fiscal lever the government would have at its disposal to push the economy toward full employment or to maintain it there. This budget would cover investment activities that could be accelerated or decelerated according to the general state of business. Because of the possibly long lag between the decision to intervene and the implementation of the investment plan, the government should have plans in the shelf ready for action at the first signs that the economy might be cooling off.[9] The pace of these investments would be set according to the need of sustaining aggregate demand, although Keynes did admit that there might be technical difficulties in the way of such changes of pace.[10]

Similar investment-plans-on-the-shelf should be kept by local governments and the semi-autonomous public bodies Keynes had already mentioned in the 1920s, also to be put in action when the times demanded it. They would work in similar ways as to the capital budget, with some possible advantages however in terms of agility and political accountability.

Fiscal policy could also contribute to increase demand through redistributive programs which could push aggregate consumption upwards. Keynes was very creative in devising reform programs to redistribute income and wealth, the boldest of which was the compulsory loans proposed at the beginning of World War II.[11]

The examination of the measures themselves should not divert our attention from the essential point that their success is not to be measured by the volume of investments actually made by the government, let alone by the volume of *deficit spending* made. Ideally, *fiscal intervention is successful if it can show private agents that the government is capable of intervening efficiently, when necessary, to support aggregate demand*. In practice, fiscal policy stance would be shown by the volume of intended government spending, not by budget deficits. The capital budget could find itself in deficit, but deficit-spending is *not* an instrument, it is a *result*, contingent on the behavior of many variables, including tax revenues. Given the tax structure of a country, tax revenues depend on the intensity and speed with which the economy responds to the stimulus represented by the increase in investment made by government. It is thus the expenditure that matters as an instrument of fiscal policy, not whether it is deficit spending. Again ideally, fully successful fiscal policy, in Keynes's sense, would convince private agents that aggregate incomes could be sustained by government intervention, reducing their uncertainties and inducing them to activate their own investment plans. In this sense, paradoxically, a completely successful expenditure plan could, in fact, never have to be implemented! Besides, even if implemented, it could generate enough tax revenues to fund it. Only if private expectations were unmoved by such initiatives, and private agents reacted with less than full confidence on the ability of government to steer aggregate demand, the impact of the policy on income would be subdued and a budget deficit would emerge. Given the tax structure and the relevant multipliers, government spending could be set to generate precisely the amount of tax revenues that would fund it without any deficit emerging.

Deficit spending was thus a *last resort* instrument. In Keynes's words:

> ... if, for one reason or another, the volume of planned investment fails to produce equilibrium, the lack of balance would be met by unbalancing one way or the other the current Budget. *Admittedly this would be a last resort, only to come into play if the machinery of capital budgetting (sic) had broken down.*
>
> (CW 27: 352, my emphasis)[12]

Keynes also raised the possibility of influencing private investment, but, as Wilson (1982) pointed out, it is not clear how this could be done beyond the general stimulus represented by an increase in aggregate demand. In particular, Keynes's reference to a desired degree of socialization of investment has been an enduring enigma. For some, it related to the creation of the "semi-autonomous public bodies," something like public companies, to promote investments even when it could not be attractive to private entrepreneurs. For others, like Tobin, Keynes could be thinking of the kind of planning that came to be adopted in France after the war (Tobin, 1987: 8). *Indicative planning*, as it was called, consisted in orienting and stimulating private investment towards specific areas targeted for development. Seeking voluntary adhesion on the part of private firms, it contrasted to the compulsory planning of command economies, which Keynes abhorred.

Monetary policy

For some critics, Keynes's contribution to economic policy consisted in showing that money does not matter and that only fiscal policy can effectively influence aggregate demand.[13] The criticism was undoubtedly fair when directed to some (but not all) of the leading members of the American Keynesian school, known as neoclassical synthesis Keynesians, like Lawrence Klein. It was completely misdirected if Keynes himself was the target, though.

Keynes devoted most of his professional life to devising monetary arrangements, institutions and policies that could contribute to reaching and maintaining full employment and price stability. It is, in any case, true that after the GT his conception of an *activist* monetary policy became something of a paradox. In short, he proposed that to be effective, monetary policy had to be used sparingly. Keynes argued that interest rates are essentially *conventional*. People are supposed to form a view as to what is the *normal* rate of interest and to expect that actual rates gravitate around that level. Those who judge the actual rate to be higher than the normal rate will take measures to anticipate a future fall of the interest rate. Those evaluating that the current rate is below the normal rate will act in anticipation of a future rise of the interest rate. It is through the anticipation of expected movements of the rates of interest that monetary policy acts. Of course, as already discussed extensively in this book, in Keynes's view, *normal* rates had nothing to do with *natural* rates of interest or any concept of this kind. Normality is a subjective concept in the sense that it is an elaboration made by each individual based on his or her own experience. Divergence of opinion as to what is normal is in fact an essential element of Keynes's liquidity preference theory of interest rates.

Be as it may, people are influenced by what they see in the markets when forming their idea of what is normal. For this reason, an employment-stabilizing monetary policy should inform the public that normal rates *are* low and *will continue to be* low in the future. Otherwise, when cheap money was needed, the monetary authorities could find it difficult to keep actual rates low, because the public would anticipate its rise to the expected "normal" level later, that is, low rates would not be seen as a durable configuration but as a *temporary* deviation of normally higher rates. If that is the case, bears will hold money, in anticipation of the expected rise in the interest rate, and the actual interest rate will remain higher than desired by the monetary authority. To avoid all this, Keynes proposed that the authorities should keep rates *permanently* low, to avoid the emergence of "bearish sentiment" which pushes interest rates up and aggregate spending down. If a contraction of aggregate demand is necessary (to fight profit inflation, for instance), other means to achieve it must be found, avoiding any rise in the rate of interest (CW 21, Chapter 5; Keynes 1977).

Monetary arrangements should be designed to permit monetary authorities to pursue the policies they consider adequate to *national* objectives, without being restrained by external obstacles (CW 26: 19). This freedom was actually reached by Great Britain in the 1930s, after the collapse of the gold standard and the accumulation of foreign reserves. Under those circumstances, Keynes stated,

> If we know what rate of interest is required to make profitable a flow of new projects at the proper pace, we have the power to make that rate prevail in the market.
>
> (Keynes 1977: 73)[14]

An important condition for this power to be exercised was the government to avoid to impose its own liquidity preferences on the public. The kinds of securities that had be issued to cover fiscal deficits should be designed to satisfy the demand by the public. That way the government would avoid offering higher interest rates on debt securities to compensate the desire of the public for more liquid types of security.[15]

One interesting aspect of Keynes's monetary policy was his discussion of the need for secrecy in the decision-making process of the monetary authority. Contrary to what seems to have become conventional wisdom among orthodox writers, Keynes defended openness, not secrecy, as a condition for monetary policy to be effective (CW 20: 158, 262–263). A monetary economy could settle down on any one of many possible equilibrium states. Authorities should signal to agents which position was targeted. The clearer the government's directions, the quicker and smoother should be the transition to the desired position.[16]

Price and wage policies

The maintenance of high levels of aggregate demand would obviously increase the risk of emergence of inflationary pressure. Again, contrary to a widely-held view, Keynes was not oblivious to it. Already in *A Treatise on Money*, Keynes had discussed the possibility of what he called income inflation, caused by increases in efficiency wages.[17] Under full employment, Keynes believed cost pressures to be harder to contain than demand pressures (CW 27: 417). Keynes devised means to ensure that also in this front uncertainties could be reduced by concerted action.

Two lines of attack were devised. On the one hand, one had to deal with the possibility of cost pressures arising from fluctuations in the prices of raw materials. These prices tended to fluctuate, in an amplified way, with the business cycle. On the other hand, specific arrangements had to be developed to deal with the problem of money wages.

As to raw materials, Keynes argued that an international stabilization fund should be created to dampen price fluctuations, containing them within pre-set intervals. The goal was to reduce the short-term volatility of prices seeking to maintain a certain degree of stability around their long-term levels (CW 27: 114).[18] To stabilize prices, buffer stocks would be accumulated (CW 27: 121), financed by another of Keynes's proposed new institutions, the International Clearing Union. The fund would buy or sell commodities to limit price variations to intervals within which supply and demand would settle at a given price (CW 27: 116). If pressures emerged that could not be handled by the fund, quotas should be imposed (CW 27: 118–119).

As to wages, things looked more difficult. The determination of money wages involved much more than just economic elements. In the GT, Keynes showed himself to be very skeptical about the efficiency of market mechanisms to determine wages. Under sustained full employment, things would be even more difficult in this front, because "[t]he task of keeping efficiency wages reasonably stable … is a political rather than an economic problem" (CW 26: 38). Full employment policies would certainly increase the political power of workers. Devising wages policies was sure to be very difficult. Discussing the issue during the war, when full employment had been achieved and the rise of inflationary pressures was a distinct possibility, Keynes observed:

> It is obvious that wage policy raises far-reaching psychological and political issues. It can only be handled by a simple, *trustful* and imaginative policy which covers a wider field than technical finance.
>
> (CW 22: 223)

Keynes recognized that the use of incomes policy to stabilize money incomes should involve some kind of *quid pro quo*:

> The standstill of wage rates, etc. could be accompanied by other measures aimed at making the programme as a whole socially just and politically acceptable. [Again] The choice of such measures is mainly a psychological and political problem ...
>
> (CW 22: 261)

For many of Keynes's followers, including neo-classical synthesis Keynesians, incomes policies had to be a natural complement of stabilization policies.[19] It is not entirely clear whether Keynes would have proposed permanent incomes policies and of what kind. Awareness of the difficulties involved in outlining wage policies led Keynes to often propose action to contain prices exactly to prevent them from provoking wage rises that would be much harder to control (CW 22: 7, 9). Nevertheless, it is reasonable safe to assume Keynes saw some kind of incomes policy as part of the required arsenal in a monetary economy. At least once Keynes had the opportunity to indicate his preference for something other than just leaving wage setting to market mechanisms. Discussing the deflationary consequences of Great Britain's return to the gold standard in the mid-1920s, Keynes concluded:

> The truth is that we stand midway between two theories of economic society. The one theory maintains that wages should be fixed by what is "fair" and "reasonable" as between classes. The other theory – the theory of the economic juggernaut – is that wages should be settled by economic pressure, otherwise called "hard facts," and that our vast machine should crash along, with regard only to its equilibrium as a whole, and without attention to the chance consequences to individual groups.
>
> (CW 9: 223–224)

Needless to say, Keynes subscribed to the first of these theories.

Other policies

Keynes contributed to the discussion of policy choices in many areas, as did practically all of his followers. The principle of concerted action is certainly not exhausted by the consideration of demand and price policies. Although industrial policies were never the main focus of Keynes's attention, and despite his aversion to intervention in allocation matters, he did warn against the idealization of the functioning of markets and of the price system when dealing with the problem of whether or not to stimulate certain sectors of the economy. Keynes argued that comparative advantages were not extensible to manufacture (CW 26: 262–263, 264), and prices themselves could not always be good indices of social needs (CW 26: 288).[20] Respect for the operation of markets did not exclude the appeal to instruments like the imposition of import quotas and controls on the circulation of financial capital when circumstances required.

Exchange rate policies, on the other hand, qualified as macroeconomic policy and were a lifelong interest of Keynes's. He authored many blueprints for reforms, including the Bancor Plan presented at the Bretton Woods conference. Again, reduction of uncertainties and the promotion of employment through the creation of an elastic supply of international means of payment were at the center of his concerns. The ideal system should combine the drive to create a situation where national authorities could have autonomy to pursue full employment policies with initiatives to coordinate actions to stabilize international trade and capital movements. Rules and flexibility to adapt were the passwords. The rules devised by Keynes in the Bancor Plan would impose the sharing of responsibilities for the elimination of imbalance of payments disequilibria between debtor and creditor countries instead of laying all the burden of adjustment on the shoulders of the former. Besides, it would establish fixed, but adjustable, exchange rates. Its most distinctive feature, perhaps, was the creation of an international means of payment, the *bancor*, a type of scriptural money to be used exclusively by central banks. An International Clearing Union would manage the international payments system, as a bank, issuing bancors when international trade was expanding. In case of need, countries would enjoy credit facilities put at their disposal by the ICU, financed by the balances of surplus countries, to go through temporary disequilibria in their balance of payments or to gain breathing space while implementing more fundamental adjustments in their external positions. This was a crucial element of Keynes's plan. It would substitute the *banking principle*, that allows endogenous liquidity and credit expansion, for the hoarding of foreign exchange reserves, with its contractionary consequences on economic activity.

5 Conclusion

We had two goals in this chapter. First, we wanted to demonstrate that there is in effect an interventionist bias in Keynes's macroeconomics. This bias is the result both of his view on how the uncertainties that plague private economic activity in modern capitalist economies impact the level of activity and of his own aprioristic beliefs about the possibility of the state conducting successful intervention in the economy. This was supported by the argument that the main problem to be faced by policy makers in an entrepreneurial economy is not how to improve upon the allocation of resources obtained by private agents but to induce the full mobilization of resources. Volume, not the direction, of utilized factors of production was the problem.

Second, we wanted to identify the main policy strategies and instruments that are compatible with the objective of maintaining full employment in an economy prone to episodes of deficient aggregate demand.

We proposed in this chapter that Keynes's stand as to the need for macroeconomic policy, on its turn, results from two sets of assumptions. First, the concept of monetary or entrepreneurial economy is marked by the possibility of aggregate demand failure because of the possibility that private agents will prefer to accumulate liquid, non-reproducible assets instead of labor-using real capital assets. Second, governments are able to assess the nature of these failures and to effectively compensate the deficiency of private aggregate demand through their own demand management policies.

Two points should be made clear, at this point. First, that the policies and policy instruments examined in this chapter represent a minimum set of goals and means of intervention compatible with Keynes's diagnosis of deficiencies of aggregate demand as the most important difficulty faced by modern entrepreneurial economies. They do not represent a closed set of instruments. Even the insistence on the need of concerted policy action in many areas made in the chapter does not mean that the instruments to be used are necessarily those listed in the appropriate sections. Policy making does not reflect exclusively "scientific" prescriptions of medicines to be applied to a sick economy. It also reflects, to variable extents, preferences of analysts, politicians, policy makers and general society through public opinion. "Left wing" Keynesians may prefer strategies and policy instruments that are more intrusive than Keynes actually considered adequate. Many of his followers may not share his Marshallian belief that markets can be efficient to promote the proper allocation of social resources. Certainly many of his followers will also disagree about the extent of social inequality that may be acceptable in modern societies or about the tradeoffs between pursuing price stabilization and full employment in situations where policies to pursue the two objectives may conflict.[21] Even when the objective is generally agreed, Keynesians can still disagree on the specific means to pursue them.[22]

Second, since this is an area where economics overlaps with politics, it is important not to forget that modes of state intervention go beyond the limits set in this chapter. In particular, social reform in one direction or another has to be also considered. Moreover, policy views and proposals will probably reflect longer views of the "economic problem" than that restricted to macroeconomic stability, however important the latter may be (and undoubtedly it really is). Views as to what constitutes the "good society" will influence the choice of policies as much as more permanent forms of state intervention in the economy (both to increase it or to decrease it). These questions, however, go much beyond the limits of a study such as this.[23]

Notes

1 In terms of domestic policies, many of these documents are collected in CW 27. Pioneers in the examination of the material are Kregel (1983) and Wilson (1982).
2 Outside the private sector whole rules of behavior and material possibilities are described in the concept of entrepreneurial economy.
3 See, for instance, Hayek (1949), particularly Chapter 4.
4 "I have not abandoned the view that something like free enterprise can be made to work" (CW 27: 354).

5 One could remember, for instance, Keynes's interventions in the debate on the future of the coal industry in the twenties, and, more particularly, his discussion of commercial policy to be adopted after the war was over. See CW 19 and 26, respectively, for each of these debates.

6 Again, this did not preclude industrial policies from influencing allocation when deemed wise. The point is that it would not be a *macroeconomic* policy, anyway.

7 See, for instance, CW 27: 264 ss, particularly p. 269.

8 This section is heavily influenced by Kregel (1983). See also Wilson (1982). The author has explored some of these arguments in Cardim de Carvalho (1992), Chapter 12.

9 As the prince of Denmark once put it, "the readiness is all" (act 5, scene 2). This point seemed to be inspired to Keynes by criticisms received from Treasury officials in the 1930s. See Peden (2004).

10 See CW 27: 322, and also pp. 122 and 268.

11 See "How to Pay for the War," in CW 9. Keynes's proposals generated an intense debate with academic colleagues, government officials and trade union leaders. As a result of these controversies, Keynes made many improvements to his original proposal, changing its character from a price stabilization program to a wealth redistribution program. See CW 22. Keynes also welcomed the recommendations contained in the Beveridge Report to reform social security with "wild enthusiasm" (CW 27: 204, 215, 225). These programs and reactions, and Keynes's political and social vision underlying them, were examined in Cardim de Carvalho (2008).

12 Keynes completed his reasoning as follows: "Thus the capital budgeting is a method of maintaining equilibrium; the deficit budgeting is a means of attempting to cure disequilibrium if and when it arises" (CW 27: 352–353).

13 See, for instance, Buchanan (1987: 132–134)

14 The validity of the statement was conditional on certain features of the period:

> With the existing control over the exchanges which has revolutionized the technical position, and with the vast resources at the disposal of the authorities through the Bank of England, the Exchange Equalization Fund, and other funds under the control of the Treasury, *it lies within their power*, by the exercise of the moderation, the gradualness, and the discreet handling of the market of which they have shown themselves to be masters, *to make the long-term rate of interest what they choose within reason.*
>
> (Keynes 1977: 73, my emphasis)

Keynes repeated the statement in 1945, now without so many preconditions: "The monetary authorities can have any rate of interest they like" (CW 27: 390). To guarantee national autonomy in monetary policy setting was one of the central goals of the Keynes Plan presented at the 1944 Bretton Woods Conference (CW 25). Keynes's proposals were, however, defeated and the American plan was adopted instead. One should remember, anyway, that Keynes was favorable to the permanent maintenance of controls on exchanges and on the movement of capital after the war.

15 See CW 21, Chapter 21; CW 22: 414; and CW 27: 392.

16 Modern orthodox economists, on other hand, believe that market economies tend to move spontaneously towards a uniquely determined equilibrium position, the one corresponding to the natural rate of unemployment. In this case, governments can only move the economy away from that position by misleading them into thinking that the foundations for their decisions are different from what they really are. Secrecy as to the true nature of such policies becomes, therefore, a condition for its effectiveness.

17 Not to be confused with the usage more recently made of the expression by, for instance, New Keynesians. Keynes used efficiency wages to refer to a specific quotient between the money wage unit and the output produced by a unit of labor. Efficiency wage is, thus, a measure of the labor cost of production.

18 Since many developing countries depend directly on the export revenues of raw materials, the fund would also contribute to stabilize international trade, by smoothing out those countries' incomes.

19 See, for instance, Weintraub (1978) and Tobin (1985: 116).

20 As Keynes wrote in this occasion to Marcus Fleming: "I did not say that you should not be attached to the price system. (I share your attachment) I said you should not be deceived by it" (CW 26: 297).

21 See Cardim de Carvalho and Lopez (2007) for a discussion of the reasons why full employment policies were abandoned even by nominally progressive governments around the 1990s.

22 It is famous the conflict that opposed "left wing" Keynesians like John Kenneth Galbraith to "right wing" Keynesians like Walter Heller in the choice of expansionary instruments to fight the recession of the United States economy during the first year of John F. Kennedy's administration. Heller defended tax reductions against Galbraith's proposal to expand government expenditures. It was believed that tax reductions were socially regressive while government expenditure, if directed at socially disadvantaged groups, could be the opposite. For the wide variety of views as to what the qualification "Keynesian" means, see Hall (1989) and Wattel (1985), a small sample among a vast literature.

23 We did discuss, however, the "social" view of Keynes, which certainly informs at least some of his policy proposals, in Cardim de Carvalho (2008).

9 Conclusion

Liquidity preference theory and the great recession

1 Introduction

At the end of the day, the value of economic theories should not be measured by their intricacies or by the cleverness of their proponents. For economics, as for any other discipline, the proof of the pudding is in the eating. Theories must be capable of explaining actual historical processes and, whenever is the case, of suggesting efficient means of intervention to improve the lives of individuals. Economic theories are instruments to obtain knowledge about concrete situations, not an end in themselves, and obviously it cannot be different with Keynesian economics or the variant of Keynesian theories that was proposed in this book, based on the prominence of liquidity preference theory.

One difficulty liquidity preference theory has to face in this particular aspect is that its predictions are hardly observable during *normal* times, let alone prosperous periods, such as cyclical upswings.[1] Wealth holders *do not prefer liquidity* when things go well and uncertainty is low. Of course, liquidity preference theory does predict that, under these conditions, demand will be strong for high-earning assets, even if they are highly illiquid, but other theories would also predict the same strong demand without consideration for liquidity premia. It is only during downswing periods, and, among them, those serious enough to make uncertainty about the future to weigh heavily on decision-makers, that liquidity considerations become clearly dominant. When things go well and are believed to continue going well there is no need to worry about emergency exits, as those provided by liquidity. This makes it easy for critics to neglect liquidity preferences, not necessarily because the theory is false, but simply because it seems irrelevant. Not only orthodox theories, such as those relying on the efficient market hypothesis, but also heterodox approaches, like those derived from Kaldor's views on money, completely neglect liquidity considerations. The same view seems to have been shared, at least until quite recently, by regulators as illustrated by the almost complete lack of references to liquidity requirements in key regulatory documents such as Basel II.

The financial crisis initiated in early 2007 in the United States, however, changed this picture dramatically.[2] In fact, in rare occasions a social theory can be exposed to such a meaningful empirical "test" as liquidity preference theory had been since 2007. Although this concluding chapter is not the place to conduct a rigorous examination of the theory advanced in this book, one can safely make the case that even a cursory examination of developments since the collapse of the subprime mortgage sector of the United States financial system strongly suggests the validity of Keynes's approach, as developed by the authors discussed in the preceding chapters. In this chapter, we intend to show that, broadly, that is, pending the necessary more rigorous investigation, a description of the main events that characterized the crisis initiated in 2007 offers strong comfort to liquidity preference theory, as has been witnessed by the large number of writers that came to rediscover not only Keynes's writings but also of some of his followers, most notably perhaps Hyman Minsky.

2 Antecedents of the 2007–2008 Financial Crisis

A complex social phenomenon such as a major economic and social crisis like the one marking the period since 2007 has many roots, some more distant, some more proximate. Where to begin, to some extent, is an arbitrary choice between digging too deep (which makes causality lines excessively thin) or too close to the surface (giving too much weight to elements that perhaps would not really deserve it just because they can be more easily related to the result one wants to explain). A reasonable starting point for the present argument is the process of financial liberalization initiated in the late 1970s, which gathered particular momentum in the 1980s and 1990s. This was a period in which important financial innovations were introduced in parallel with the structural changes resulting from the liberalization process itself. Moreover, it was also a period of great changes in dominant political views around the world about the role of the state. In the Western world, the social-democratic consensus that dominated the post war period lost terrain to conservative ideas. Reaganite and Thatcherite political groups emerged everywhere to defend a retrenchment of the state and the liberation of the energies of "free markets," particularly in the form of deregulation of markets, including financial markets, and of a cut in government expenditures.

For many financial sectors, among which the banking sector, deregulation meant the removal of constraints on balance sheet choices devised to prevent the sector from implementing investment and financing strategies that could increase financial fragility. Liberalization, however, was double-edged. On the one hand, banks and other financial firms were given much more latitude in choosing assets and liabilities and greater freedom to pursue profit-maximizing strategies. These entities would no longer be confined to specific segments of the market as before, being able to seek earning opportunities wherever they found them. The downside of liberalization was the intensification of competitive pressures on the same entities. As they were freed to penetrate other financial segments, the protection they themselves enjoyed against competitors in the form of regulatory barriers to entry also crumbled.

Competitive pressures in the 1990s and 2000s increased within a frame of falling interest rates. After the acceleration of the 1970s and the monetary shocks of the end of that decade and early 1980s, inflation rates fell dramatically all over the world and have remained low ever since. In such circumstances, policy interest rates went down and remained at very low levels as well.

Such a combination of low interest rates and heightened competitive pressures led banks and other financial institutions to seek to increase their profits at the higher risk end of the risk/return spectrum. Leveraging up their purchases, they could buy more and more of these assets, on their own account and for clients' accounts. The increase in the volume of financial operations contributed to increase the liquidity of many classes of assets, including securities that perhaps would not be considered liquid otherwise. Risky securities were considered to be safe because they were liquid. Being liquid they were sought for both for yields and for their liquidity premium, strengthening their demand. This virtuous(!) circle favored increased negotiations with these securities which, in turn, increased their liquidity, and so on.

The increased liquidity of those securities also allowed banks and others to increase their profitability by exploiting yield curve opportunities. As it happens with any class of liquid securities they could be generally accepted as collateral supporting overnight or short-term borrowing. Again, this allowed increasing leverage, reinforcing the circle described above.

But which were these securities that could remunerate holders well while also offering high liquidity premia? A large share of the supply of securities that satisfied those demands were a result of the push to securitization that was going on since the late 1980s. Practically any contract that offered the perspective of regular future flows of repayment became a candidate for securitization.[3] Commercial and residential mortgages, student loans, credit card payments were among the types of debt most frequently securitized. In its ideal concept, such a security would allow the original lender to recover the value of the loan plus its income much more quickly than would be the case were he to wait until repayment at the contracted dates. On the other hand, for the buyer, these securities were no different from any other financial asset. In fact, it could in theory improve the choices available to the investor since different types of underlying loans would be reflected in different payoff characteristics of the securitized asset.

The wide market created for securitized debt, however, masked its actual risk characteristics, because its high liquidity gave to investors (and to financial institutions) a false assurance of safety. The system as a whole was becoming steadily more illiquid as practices such as securitization advanced.[4] As discussed in Chapter 3, liquidity premia of privately-created assets may disappear as easily and quickly as it can be created. As long as financial institutions and investors trusted that markets could absorb indefinitely large amounts of such assets at more or less constant prices, those markets would remain liquid and expectations would be largely self-fulfilling. As returns offered by many among securitized assets were also very attractive, they seemed to be an impossible to refuse proposition. Rising demands seemed to feed further rises in demand, enough to absorb new issuance of those securities, and so on.

Systemic illiquidity, however, could be diagnosed from two sets of data. First, *private liquidity* was expanding, but *ultimate liquidity*, as defined by Minsky[5], was rising at much lower rates. As discussed before, this is not a problem as long as the public may trust that privately created liquid assets can effectively be converted in ultimate liquidity at any time. Second, balance sheet illiquidity was rising, as leverage and maturity mismatches between assets and liabilities were continuously raised.[6] In Hyman Minsky's terms, financial fragility was growing as financial investors and institutions became less and less capable of absorbing even relatively minor adverse shocks.

The collection of such sets of data faces non-trivial difficulties, even for countries with such an extensive data availability such as the United States. Existing data bases were *not* designed with concerns similar to those of Minsky's. Aggregate data about maturity mismatches are not, as far as I know, available. It is possible to give a rough estimate of such mismatches for individual institutions, by calculating the ratios short- and long-term assets and liabilities but it would still be a poor proxy to the actual index proposed by Minsky.

The ratio between ultimate and total liquidity, however, can be estimated with more confidence. Minsky suggested that ultimate liquidity would include practically all assets issued on government's authority. Thus, it would include not only government-issued currency but also public debt securities issued by the central government. But many of these securities are variable in value. Therefore, a more restricted set of assets, however, may be a better indication of what constitutes ultimate liquidity. Graph 1 presents the evolution in recent decades of the value of government-created money, the monetary base, and a variable representing private liquidity in the United States. Private liquidity was estimated

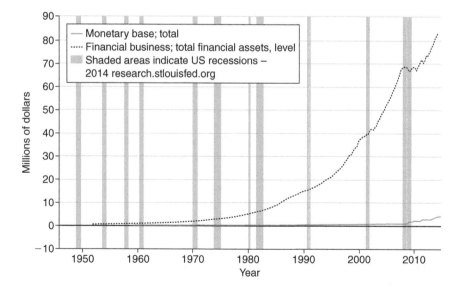

Figure 9.1 Total value of financial assets of financial institutions and monetary base.

using the total value of financial assets held by financial institutions. This number certainly overestimates to some degree the value of private liquidity, because some financial assets are held for purposes other than serving as a liquidity reserve. Nevertheless, in the last two to three decades, the liquidity premium associated to all classes of financial assets became more and more important to investors, so that it was enhanced in many securities, either through the development of secondary markets or similar institutions, or through the attachment of derivatives to those assets intended to work as a convertibility substitute.

In the graph, we can see the acceleration of the growth of the value of financial assets held by financial institutions, while the monetary base only grew more rapidly *after* the crisis had began, as a result of the Federal Reserve policies to increase liquidity. Private liquidity growth stopped in the first years after the financial crisis began in the United States, but has resumed growth more recently.

As it is well known, the shock came in the form of a collapse in a segment of the residential mortgage securitized debt market. Mortgage-Backed Securities (MBS for short) created on the basis of subprime mortgages were the most egregious example of how financial techniques and innovation might eventually serve no other purpose than misleading buyers of financial assets. But this is not the most important point in the attempt to understand the financial crisis initiated in 2007. If Minsky's financial fragility model, which is a central piece of liquidity preference theory, is correct, even if no subprime mortgages were contracted or had been securitized, the increasing exposure to balance sheet illiquidity risks resulting from increasing leverage and maturity mismatches would have made a crisis unavoidable.[7]

In the GT, referring to "normal" business cycles, Keynes observed that the wave-like movement typical of capitalist dynamics "is mainly due to the way in which the marginal efficiency of capital fluctuates" (CW 7: 313). He also added that "[l]iquidity-preference, except those manifestations of which are associated with increasing trade and speculation, does not increase until *after* the collapse in the marginal efficiency of capital" (ibid., 316, Keynes's emphasis). Because of Keynes's expectation that a collapse of real investments should precede difficulties in money and financial markets, some commentators have argued that the current crisis is a Minsky crisis, not a Keynes crisis.

In fact, for Minsky *major* crises begin with a financial crash, more or less independently of what may be going on with respect to the marginal efficiency of capital. It is the sudden realization of balance sheet illiquidity induced by an adverse shock that leads wealth holders to try to access ultimate liquidity sources to strengthen their positions.[8] If credit lines are congested, there is only one way left to the individual to recover liquidity, that is, selling assets, or "to sell position to make position," a phrase often attributed to Minsky. If the shock hit a sufficiently large number of wealth-holders, however, the demand for liquidity obviously cannot be satisfied since there will be nobody to sell to.[9] Asset prices then will fall freely, in Minsky's version of Fisher's debt deflation, until financial wealth is so completely destroyed that there is nothing more to sell. The destruction of financial wealth would affect not only individual wealth holders, but also banks and other financial institutions, anybody who kept financial assets in their balance sheets. Credit lines would dry out and consumption and investment would crash, leading the economy to a depression, that is, a prolonged state of prostration like the one experienced in the 1930s, with all its risks and consequences.

A depression, however, is not pre-determined. Government authorities can intervene to prevent a debt deflation, since they have the power to create the ultimate liquidity that is demanded by private wealth holders. The authorities can also support aggregate demand to prevent the collapse of markets for goods and services and the rise of mass unemployment, if they pursue enlightened macroeconomic policies.

3 The financial crisis

As the financial crisis initiated in 2007 in the United States recedes in time, an increasing number of factual descriptions of its actual events has been made available.[10] One can choose among alternative narratives of the crisis centered on individual banks or segments of the US financial system, on sectors, on the actions of the Federal Government or the Federal Reserve, or even on the strategies implemented by some individuals, among other choices.

The trigger for the crisis was the realization that expectations of return from purchases of subprime Mortgage-Backed Securities (MBS) had been grossly overestimated. *Subprime mortgages* has become a familiar expression all over the world. It refers to mortgage loans made to households who did not fulfill practically any of the safety requirements listed by Fannie Mae and Freddie Mac as preconditions to qualify for their support. Being riskier loans, subprime mortgage loans could charge higher interest rates (although the determination of interest rates in these contracts followed complex paths). But the risk/return tradeoffs were masked by some ingenious devices that securitization had made possible. First, the packaging and tranching of large number of loans into new securities made them more opaque for investors. The (perhaps) active connivance of credit rating agencies gave these securities very high marks, including triple A in many cases reassuring financial investors as to the safety of these assets.

But opacity was not the whole story. More fundamentally, the success of subprime MBS was based on the expectation that house prices would keep going up, if not forever, at least for a long time in the future. As long as house prices went up, loan non-performance could be dealt with without major problems. The mortgaged house could be sold, allowing to debt to be paid and even, perhaps, leaving something of a residual capital gain to the borrower. Of course, any financial scheme the return of which depends on the continuous increase in prices of the underlying asset is a Ponzi scheme. It follows the "bicycle principle": it can only survive while demand keeps rising at the necessary rates to guarantee that the relevant price would increase enough to keep the scheme attractive to new participants. Securitization allowed mortgage lenders to renew their loans much more quickly than would be the case had they had to wait until debt liquidation by borrowers to recover their funds. New rounds of mortgage financing would add fuel to the rise in house prices, thereby confirming the expectations that led to those operations and stimulating their expansion. The intense pace of negotiation of such assets created the market liquidity necessary to reassure MBS buyers that they could always sell them or use them to get loans if unexpected problems emerged. The active market for MBS, therefore, signaled to investors that the liquidity premium attached to such securities was very high. Again, such predictions are self-fulfilling as long as they last.

For whatever reason, however, this feedback process began to lose steam by the end of 2006, beginning of 2007.[11] Increasing non-performance forced rating agencies to downgrade some securities. Wealth holders' enthusiasm for MBS fell and with it both market liquidity and funding liquidity also fell. Some high profile cases of financial institutions which found themselves unable to maintain their extreme leverage levels and maturity mismatches between assets and liabilities, like the investment bank Bear Stearns, or of banks that accumulated what began to be called "toxic" assets in their balance sheets, added to the atmosphere of rising uncertainty.

Under these conditions, opacity, which had helped to expand the market when expectations were favorable, acted in the opposite direction. Uncertain about which loans were securitized into the assets they bought, investors tended to dump all of them. Some of them did it as liquidity preference rose, because no one could know what was in store even for the immediate future. Others did it because they anticipated further losses in MBS values and wanted to get out before it actually happened (a strategy that is usually doomed from the start). Finally, some did it, as it was the case of investment banks, because they relied on very short-term (sometimes overnight) funding to maintain their MBS portfolios and found out they could not renew the loans they needed.[12]

Debt deflation, at this point, was more than a possibility, it was a process already in its first steps of development. In fact, contagion soon took place, hitting other Asset Backed Securities. Uncertain about the identification of loans that were packaged in each security issue, Asset-Backed Securities holders in general began to dump them in the markets. Prices fell, hitting even those institutions and entities which decided to hold on to their securities and wait, since most of them are subject to mark-to-market evaluation systems.

At this point, general illiquidity could lead to general insolvency, with all its longer-term consequences. If the fall in prices of assets was sharp enough, it could reduce the value of assets below that of liabilities by a larger margin than that constituted by the net worth of the investor. The snowball effect on financial assets prices was contained, however, by the action of the United States Treasury Department and the Federal Reserve.[13] The intervention was successful in stopping debt deflation but it was not timely enough to prevent contagion to the "real" side of the economy.[14]

A central channel of contagion was the rise in the liquidity preference of banks, in ways similar to those witnessed in the 1930s. The enlarged provision of "ultimate liquidity" by Federal authorities could stop the fire sales that fed debt deflation by restoring market liquidity for the surviving securities but it could not, *per se*, restore financial flows to non-financial sectors, that is, to increase what Keynes called "advances to customers" to feed industrial circulation. In fact, liquidity tended to be concentrated on banks in the form of reserves with monetary authorities throughout most of the period. As Table 1 shows, accumulation of excess reserves by banks survived even the reduction and eventual removal of its (already low) remuneration, while credit to private borrowers, particularly for business, still has not recovered its pre-crisis level.

By the end of June 2014, seven years after the financial crisis began, and five after the recession was declared "over" by the NBER, banks still maintained reserves amounting to US$2,668 *trillion*, when required reserves amounted to slightly less than US$90 *billion*.[15]

4 Contagion to Western Europe

A few large European banks were hit by the subprime crisis practically at the same time than American banks, since they had also invested in those securities. Problems with British, German and Swiss banks forced the national authorities of those countries to act to prevent any snowballing effect to be reproduced in the region more or less at the same time in which American authorities were trying to stop the financial downward spiral in the US.

A more serious threat, however, would come later. Rising liquidity preference of lenders, particularly banks, after the near-death experience of 2007 and 2008 led to a worldwide retrenchment of the financial system. A "flight to safety" took place in the form of a fall in the demand for all kinds of assets except those perceived as exceptionally strong and liquid, such as public debt securities of a few countries, most notably the United States. Yields on US Treasury securities fell to record lows and remained there. Not even the political conflicts around fiscal policy choices and public debt limits in the United States was enough to convince asset holders to shift their demand toward other assets. Neither did the downgrading of Treasury securities, proposed by a major credit rating agency, lead to any perceptible change in demand. Safety and liquidity considerations seem to have overwhelmed all other arguments in the mind of investors.

Of course, US Treasury securities are favored not only by its being backed by taxing powers in the largest economy in the world, but also by their denomination in domestic currency, the US dollar, which means that bankruptcy is, for all

Table 9.1 Commercial banks in the United States

Rates of growth of cash and commercial and industrial loans (%)

	2009	2010	2011	2012	2013
Commercial and industrial loans	−18.7	−9.2	8.5	11.6	7.2
Cash	49.5	−7.8	47.6	−2.1	55.2

Source: www.federalreserve.gov/releases/h8/current/default.htm, downloaded November 11, 2014.

practical purposes, off the table. They were also supported by the existence of wide and deep secondary markets, which gives them the position of most liquid security in the world. Treasury securities are, thus, an obvious destination for the demand of liquidity-seeking investors. The three other largest economies in the world do not count on the same advantages. China is still largely a financially-closed economy. Japan has been struggling to leave behind it a semi-depression that has already lasted more than twenty years. Even the most promising competitor to the US dollar, the euro, is handicapped by the fragmentation of banking and capital markets in the eurozone.

About ten years after its creation, the euro was widely seen by the end of the first decade of the century as a success. Despite the ample differences in economic performances and opportunities of the countries that joined the euro, financial markets seemed to believe that the richest economies, notably Germany, would always be willing to come to the rescue if any individual country faced some particularly adverse situation. Balance of payments deficits could be financed without much difficulty at very low interest rates and the same occurred with fiscal deficits. Risks of financial assets issued by national governments in the eurozone seemed to have been assessed on the assumption that Germany would always work as the area's lender-of-last-resort. Interest rates were set having German risk in mind, rather than the actual risk of the country issuing the debt.

Shock waves generated by the financial crisis in the United States hit the European Union, and in particular the eurozone, through many channels. As already noted, some large banks in Europe had invested in subprime securitized assets and now had to share the losses. To avoid the collapse of their banking sectors, countries like Ireland implemented rescue packages that greatly increased their fiscal deficits in need of finance. Exports to the United States were hit by the latter's fall in income. The most important channel, however, was the impact of rising liquidity preference that led to a severe retrenchment in the credit supply. Loans became more scarce and much more expensive. As many countries in the European Union were affected more or less at the same time, it also became rapidly clear that Germany could not, or would not, act as the lender-of-last-resort in a crisis of such a scale. The premises on which financial flows were built since the early 1990s suddenly crumbled. Uncertainty rose sharply and, with it, so did liquidity preferences.

Again, in similar ways to what happens in a domestic financial crisis, the sudden realization that risk/return calculations had been based on false premises led to a pattern of reactions that entailed a cumulative disequilibrium process. Upward reevaluation of risks led to higher interest rates (or outright credit rationing) which sharpened difficulties of borrowers, which further increased risk perceptions, etc. Some countries in what became known as the periphery of the eurozone were not strong enough to survive by themselves to such a movement. Greece, Ireland, Portugal, and, much later, Cyprus, had to seek help in the form of international bailout packages.[16] Some countries, such as Spain, faced almost as tough threats as the other four, but somehow managed to survive without formally asking for help.[17] Others, like Italy, were seen to be at great risk but also did survive, even if at great macroeconomic cost. Even a pillar of the European Union and the eurozone like France had to face the skepticism of financial markets as to its chance of recovery.

5 Austerity policies

The European Union reacted to the coming of the crisis much in the same way as the most important economies in the continent did in the 1930s. Faced with mass unemployment and a steep fall in the level of activity, the recovery strategy that was pursued in the 2010s, as it had happened with France, Germany before the rise of Nazism, and Italy in the early 1930s, consisted in the adoption of *austerity* policies. The fall in output, and the accompanying rise of mass unemployment, tends to generate fiscal deficits, since revenues fall with incomes and expenditure rises with unemployment. Then, as now, there were two alternative strategies to resolve the crisis: to expand aggregate demand through public investment in order to increase income and employment; or to reduce public expenditure to balance the budget in the expectation that businessmen's confidence that taxes are not going to be raised or that irresponsible governments will not intervene in the economy will be strengthened, causing them to expand production and employment. Austerity was also a way to pursue a less popular goal: large-scale unemployment should stimulate workers to accept lower wages to keep their jobs. The fall in labor costs should raise the competitiveness of the country's export industries. The increase in foreign demand would fill the output gap created by the fall of domestic demand, as long, of course, as external demand remained stable. Under the gold standard, a fall in labor costs would allow a country to recover, although at the expense of its partners.

In the 2010s, austerity was also the recipe for macroeconomic policy adopted by the European Union. The justification for austerity was fundamentally the same. If anything, the appeal to expanding net exports was perhaps a little more open than in the past. The impact of unemployment on labor costs should, on the other hand, be strengthened by the implementation of "structural reforms" of variable content, but always containing measures to increase the "flexibility of labor markets," with particular emphasis on the removal of barriers to hiring and firing employees.[18] Cuts in state expenditure were very deep in the peripheral countries of the eurozone, as one can see from Table 9.2. In contrast, countries like Germany and France actually *increased* state expenditures.[19]

In the 2010s, as in the 1930s, austerity policies in Europe led to the same results: a steep fall in output and employment, except in countries like Germany which had in fact reduced their labor costs much before the crisis began. As to the others, some measure of stability was only recovered after a significant loss of income in some cases, while a few others, including France and Italy, still struggle to avoid heavier losses without much success. The ones where timid recoveries have been observed usually rely on the growth of net exports, which remains low and volatile anyway. GDP growth rates in the European Union, at

Table 9.2 Consumption expenditure of general government

	(Current prices, in million euro)				
	2009	*2010*	*2011*	*2012*	*2013*
Ireland	33.270	30.404	29.893	29.432	–
Greece	47.457	40.791	36.248	33.835	31.349
Portugal	37.185	37.334	34.081	30.120	31.422
Spain	223.603	224.511	222.215	207.673	205.515
Italy	324.684	327.003	321.580	313.279	310.675

Source: Eurostat: http://epp.eurostat.ec.europa.eu/tgm/table.do?tab=table&init=1&language=en&pco de=tec00010&plugin=1 downloaded November 27, 2014.

best, pointed to stagnation, at worst to double or triple dips, with recessions rearing their heads again and again (Table 9.3).

In such conditions, one cannot be surprised to find that liquidity preference remained high, particularly in the banking sector. Loans to private borrowers in the euro area after 2010 reached a peak in 2011 and fell afterwards, both to non-financial corporations and to households, as one can see in Table 9.4.

Minsky expected the memory of a financial disaster to linger on for an extended period of time. Expectations can amplify economic fluctuations making growth higher than it is justified in the upswing, but trapping the economy in a declining or stagnant state for longer than necessary. The Great Depression, as Friedman and Schwartz (1963) showed, was such a period, in large part thanks to the resistance of banks to lend to businesses and consumers, to preserve the liquidity of their positions in case runs could begin again during the 1930s decade. Banks and other financial institutions in the United States and in the European Union in the 2010s seemed to have largely followed the same strategy. To reduce leverage and increase the liquidity of their balance sheets seemed to be the main objective of those entities in recent years. Advances to customers, as

Table 9.3 Real GDP growth rates in the European Union and selected countries (%)

	2009	*2010*	*2011*	*2012*	*2013*
European Union (27 countries)	−4.5	2	1.7	−0.4	0.1
Germany	−5.1	4	3.3	0.7	0.4
France	−3.1	1.7	2	0	0.2
Italy	−5.5	1.7	0.4	−2.4	−1.9
Ireland	−6.4	−1.1	2.2	0.2	−0.3
Greece	−3.1	−4.9	−7.1	−7	−3.9
Spain	−3.8	−0.2	0.1	−1.6	−1.2
Portugal	−2.9	1.9	−1.3	−3.2	−1.4

Source: Eurostat, http://epp.eurostat.ec.europa.eu/tgm/table.do?tab=table&init=1&language=en&pco de=tec00115&plugin=1 downloaded November 27, 2014.

Table 9.4 Total loans to private sector – Euro Area

(EUR billions)

	Non-financial corporations	*Households*
out/10	4.682	5125
out/11	4.761	5321
out/12	4.643	5243
out/13	4.378	5235
out/14	4.274	5197

Source: European Central Bank, Press Release: Monetary Developments in the Euro Area, issues October 2010, October 2011, October 2012, October 2013, October 2014.

Keynes called them, seem to be too risky: it is impossible to know who is really healthy, who is really competitive, how solid are guarantees offered by potential borrowers, how far safety margins could be reduced to allow banks to increase their supply of credit.

As these remain the main features of the American and European economies some years after the financial crisis began in the United States and spread throughout the world, observable results are precisely those that the liquidity preference school would predict: semi-stagnation, with periods of low and volatile growth, maintenance of high rates of unemployment, sharpening of social problems generated not only by the rise of unemployment but also by cuts in social safety nets and social spending and finally the degradation of the political landscape, with the rise of extremist groups.[20]

The main policy implication advanced by liquidity preference theory, as, in fact, by all known Keynesian variants of economic thought is that austerity is *not* the proper strategy to achieve recovery. Managing aggregate demand to induce full employment, while preserving price stability, among other objectives, remains the Holy Grail of Keynesian economics. It is the only way to stimulate businesses to produce and to invest, maintaining activity levels and employment and accumulating capital in order to improve the lives of, potentially, everybody.

Notes

1 In fact, regular cyclical fluctuations, in the pattern observed since the end of World War II, are largely predictable and even cyclical downturns are expected and incorporated in the formation of expectations by private agents. One would expect, in these circumstances, that the liquidity preference *schedule* would remain largely stable, with changes in the demand for liquid assets responding to the variations in the expected interest rate changes, according to the speculative motive, that is, changes in the demand for money described by movements *along* the liquidity preference schedule. Cyclical fluctuations for most of the postwar period in the United States had much to do with predictable (and expected) changes in the monetary policy stance of the Federal Reserve, given its dual statutory mission to defend employment levels and the stability of the value of money. In other areas, such as Western Europe and, most

notably, Japan, for a large part of the postwar period, sustained growth was observable and cyclical fluctuations took the form of changes in the *rate* of growth. None of such movements should generate significant changes in the level of uncertainty in the sense defined by Keynes in 1937, and, therefore, no visible shifts in the liquidity preference schedule of the public.

2 The label Great Recession has been used by many analysts, to differentiate the current crisis from the Great Depression of the 1930s.

3 Securitization is a financial technique through which the rights to expected future flows of payments can be used to create a new financial asset the returns of which are constituted by those flows. The original lender can sell these newly created titles to investors, thereby anticipating to the present time the revenues he would receive in future dates.

4 Similar effects operated in the expansion of derivatives. In fact, it is not always easy to distinguish one from the other, since derivatives are defined as contracts the value of which depends on the value of another asset, and securitized assets are also created on the basis of other assets. The distinction ends up being mostly a convention rather than a difference of substance.

5 See Chapter 4, p.57.

6 Aggregate measures of maturity mismatches are hard even to conceive. There is enough anecdotal evidence, however, to strongly support the perception that this was a generalized behavior.

7 A fragility theory cannot predict when and under what precise circumstances a crisis will take place. In contrast to business cycle theories, it does not identify turning points, only the increasing probability that a turning point will be met as the shock-absorbing properties of the system become less and less efficient.

8 Again, the identification of the actual shock is of minor importance in this approach. What really matters is that the system had lost its resilience so that it may be broken for practically any reason, even those that, in more normal times, would probably pass unnoticed. This point was also emphasized by Galbraith (1997: 90). Given the extent of leverage-supported speculation in the 1920s, the identification of the trigger for the collapse in 1929 was of secondary (or lower) importance:

> This is not very important, for it is in the nature of a speculative boom that almost anything can collapse it. Any serious shock to confidence can cause sales by those speculators who have always hoped to get out before the final collapse, but after all possible gains from rising prices have been reaped.

9 If liquidity is ability to dispose of an asset, it depends on the existence of buyers when excess supply emerges. In the limit, of course, if all holders try to sell there will be no buyers and, thus, no liquidity.

10 E.g., Blinder (2013), Sorkin (2010) and Kregel (2014).

11 There are many hypotheses about what happened in that period that decelerated the price rises on which the whole scheme was based. Some observers blamed the activation of the rise in interest rates included in the clauses of contracts known as Adjustable Rates Mortgages. Others, like Blinder (2013), point to more fundamental mechanisms leading to the exhaustion of demand for houses.

12 That is, funding liquidity was also lost, not just market liquidity.

13 Blinder (2013) offers an exhaustive list of programs launched either by the Treasury or by the Fed, or by both.

14 "In total, the wealth of US households fell by something on the order of $18 *trillion*. That's more than a year's GDP" (Blinder 2013: 354).

15 Cf. the statistical release of the Federal Reserve available in www.federalreserve.gov/releases/h3/current/, downloaded on November 27, 2014.

16 For political reasons, the European Union did not want the intervention of the institution created to give help, the IMF, which could only do it, anyway, if the countries

that are its stockholders accepted to increase their contributions to its treasury. To preserve the image of an advanced region managing its own problems, a "triumvirate," which became known as *the troika*, was created, constituted by the IMF, the European Commission and the European Central Bank. The troika was to provide loans similar to the IMF's standby credits against the adoption of policy conditionalities specified by the lending institutions.

17 Spain did receive help later to support the banking system but through different mechanisms.

18 The theory behind austerity changed somehow, certainly in correspondence with the displacement of Great Britain as the leading country in the region by Germany. The British Treasury officials who led the resistance against the expansionary policies proposed, among others, by Keynes, relied for their theoretical foundations on the acceptance of Say's Law and the loanable funds theory. German proponents of austerity, in contrast, present themselves as Schumpeterian opponents of Keynesianism. See Peden (2004) for the Treasury views and Giersch (1993) for the German approach.

19 According to Eurostat, France increased consumption expenditure of general government from 467 billion euros in 2009 to 513 billion euros in 2013. See Table 2 for the source.

20 One noticeable difference between the 2010s and the 1930s is the absence of extreme left groups, after the disappearance of all but the fringe communist groups that used to populate the political system. Right-wing extremists, on the other hand, seem to be alive and well.

References

References to writings of John Maynard Keynes refer mostly to the Cambridge University Press edition, for the Royal Economic Society, of his Collected Writings, edited by Donald Moggridge and Elizabeth Johnson, published in 2012–2013. These references are identified as CW followed by volume number in arabic numerals, and, when appropriate, the page number.

Allen, F. and Gale, D. (2006). Systemic risk and regulation. Paper prepared for NBER conference on The Risks of Financial Institutions.

Bagehot, W. (1994). *Lombard Street: A Description of the Money Market*. No indication of place of publication: Dodo Press.

Barth, J., Caprio, G. and Levine, R. (2006). *Rethinking Bank Regulation. Till Angels Govern*. Cambridge: Cambridge University Press.

Bernanke, B. (2000). *Essays on the Great Depression*. Princeton: Princeton University Press.

Bibow, J. (1998). "On Keynesian theories of liquidity preference", *The Manchester School*, 66 (2), 238–273.

Blinder, A. (2013). *After the Music Stopped. The Financial Crisis, the Response, and the Work Ahead*. New York: The Penguin Press.

Buchanan, J. (1987). "Keynesian follies", in D. Reese (ed.), *The Legacy of Keynes*. San Francisco: Harper and Row.

Cardim de Carvalho, F. (1992). *Mr Keynes and the Post Keynesians. Principles of Macroeconomics for a Monetary Production Economy*. Aldershot: Edward Elgar.

Cardim de Carvalho, F. (1995). "Post Keynesian developments of liquidity preference theory", in P. Wells (ed.), *Post Keynesian Economic Theory*. Boston: Kluwer Academic Publishers.

Cardim de Carvalho, F. (1999). "On banks' liquidity preference", in P. Davidson and J. Kregel (eds), *Full Employment and Price Stability in a Global Economy*. Cheltenham: Edward Elgar.

Cardim de Carvalho, F. (2008). "Keynes and the reform of the capitalist social order", *Journal of Post Keynesian Economics*, vol. 31 (2), 191–212.

Cardim de Carvalho, F. (forthcoming), "Can Basel III work when Basel II didn't?", in D. Papadimitriou (ed.), *Contributions to Economic Theory, Policy, Development, and Finance. Essays in Honor of Jan Kregel*. London: Palgrave Macmillan.

Cardim de Carvalho, F. and Kregel, J. (2010). *What do Financial Systems and Financial Regulators Do?* Rio de Janeiro: Ibase.

Cardim de Carvalho, F. and Lopez, J. (2007). "Are full employment policies obsolete?", *International Journal of Political Economy*, vol. 36 (3), 5–23.

Davidson, P. (1978). *Money and the Real World*. 2nd edition. London: Macmillan.

Davidson, P. (1984). "Reviving Keynes's revolution", *Journal of Post Keynesian Economics*, 6 (4), 561–575, Summer.

Davidson, P. (2002). *Financial Markets, Money and the Real World*. Cheltenham: Edward Elgar.

De Bandt, O. and Hartmann, P. (2000). Systemic risk: a survey. ECB Working Paper 35, Frankfurt: European Central Bank.

Dow, S. (1997). "Endogenous money", in G. Harcourt and P. Riach (eds), *A Second Edition of The General Theory*, London: Routledge.

Dow, A. and Dow, S. (1989). "Endogenous money creation and idle balances", in J. Pheby (ed.), *New Directions in Post Keynesian Economics*. Cheltenham: Edward Elgar.

Fisher, I. (1932). *Booms and Depressions. Some First Principles*. New York: Adelphi.

Fisher, I. (1933). "The debt deflation theory of great depressions", *Econometrica*, 1 (4), 332–357.

Friedman, M. and Schwartz, A. (1963). *A Monetary History of the United States, 1867–1960*. Princeton: Princeton University Press.

Galbraith, J. K. (1997). *The Great Crash 1929*. Boston and New York: Mariner Books.

Giersch, H. (1993). *Openness for Prosperity. Essays in World Economics*. Cambridge: The MIT Press.

Goodhart, C., Hartmann, P., Llewellyn, D., Rojaz-Suarez, L. and Weisbrod, S. (1998). *Financial Regulation. Why, How and Where Now?* London: Routledge.

Goodhart, C. (2009). *The Regulatory Response to the Financial Crisis*. Cheltenham: Edward Elgar.

Gorton, G. and Winton, A. (2002). Financial intermediation. NBER Working Paper 8928.

Greenspan, A. (2010). The crisis. Available at: www.brookings.edu/~/media/Files/Programs/ES/BPEA/2010_spring_bpea_papers/spring2010_greenspan.pdf (accessed: April 27 2012).

Gurley, J. and Shaw, E. (1955). "Financial aspects of economic development", *The American Economic Review*, 45 (4), 515–538.

Hahn, F. (1984). *Equilibrium and Macroeconomics*. Cambridge: The MIT Press.

Hall, P., ed. (1989). *The Political Power of Economic Ideas. Keynesianism Across Nations*. Princeton: Princeton University Press.

Harrod, R. (1936). *The Trade Cycle: An Essay*. Oxford: The Clarendon Press.

Hayek, F. (1949). *Individualism and Economic Order*. London: Routledge and Kegan Paul.

Herring, R. and Litan, R. (1995). *Financial Regulation in the Global Economy*. New York: Brookings Institution.

Hicks, J. (1967). *Critical Essays in Monetary Theory*. Oxford: Oxford University Press.

Kahn, R. (1972). *Selected Essays on Employment and Growth*. Cambridge: Cambridge University Press.

Kahn, R. (1984). *The Making of Keynes's General Theory*. Cambridge: Cambridge University Press.

Kaldor, N. (1973a). "Monetary policy, economic stability and growth. Memoranda of evidence to the Radcliffe Commission", in A. Walters (ed.), *Money and Banking: Selected Readings*. Harmondsworth: Penguin.

Kaldor, N. (1973b). "The new monetarism", in A. Walters (ed.), cit.

Kaldor, N. (1980). *Essays on Economic Stability and Growth*. New York: Holmes and Meier Publishers, Inc.

Kaldor, N. (1986). *The Scourge of Monetarism (Radcliffe Lectures)*. 2nd edition. Oxford: Oxford University Press.

Kalecki, M. (1971). *Selected Essays on the Dynamics of the Capitalist Economy*. Cambridge: Cambridge University Press.

Kambhu, J., Schuermann, T. and Stiroh, K. (2007). "Hedge funds, financial intermediation, and systemic risk", *FRBNY Economic Policy Review*, 13 (3), 1–18.

Kaufman, G. and Scott, K. (2003). "What is systemic risk, and do bank regulators retard or contribute to it?", *The Independent Review*, 7 (3), 371–391.

Keynes, J.M. (1937). "The ex-ante theory of the rate of interest", *The Economic Journal*, 47 (188), 663–669.

Keynes, J.M. (1963). *Essays in Persuasion*. New York: W.W. Norton.

Keynes, J.M. (1977). "How to avoid a slump", Appendix to T. Hutchison, *Keynes v. the Keynesians?*. London: Institute of Economic Affairs.

Kindleberger, C. (1973). *The World in Depression: 1929–1939*. Berkeley and Los Angeles: University of California Press.

Kohn, D. (2008). Risk management and its implications for systemic risk. Testimony before the Subcommittee on Securities, Insurance and Investment, Committee of Banking, Housing, and Urban Affairs, US Senate. Available at: www.federalreserve.gov/newsevents/testimony/kohn20080619a.htm.

Kregel, J.A. (1983). "Finanziamento in disavanzo, politica economica e preferenza per la liquidità", in F. Vicarelli (ed.), *Attualità di Keynes* [Keynes's Relevance Today]. Roma-Bari: Laterza.

Kregel, J.A. (1984/85). "Constraints on the expansion of output and employment: real or monetary", *Journal of Post Keynesian Economics*, 7 (2), 139–152.

Kregel, J.A. (1988). "The multiplier and liquidity preference: two sides of the theory of effective demand", in A. Barrère (ed.), *The Foundations of Keynesian Analysis*. London: Macmillan.

Kregel, J.A. (1998). *The Past and Future of Banks*. Quaderni di Ricerche, 21, Roma: Bancaria Editrice.

Kregel, J.A. (2008). Minsky's "cushion of safety," systemic risk and the crisis in the US subprime mortgage market. The Levy Economics Institute Public Policy Brief 93.

Kregel, J. (2014). *Economic Development and Financial Instability. Selected Essays.* Edited by R. Kattel, London: Anthem Press.

Leijonhufvud, A. (1968). *On Keynesian Economics and the Economics of Keynes*. Oxford: Oxford University Press.

Leijonhufvud, A. (1981). *Information and Coordination*. Oxford: Oxford University Press.

Marx, K. (1978). *Theories of Surplus Value*, vol. II. Moscow: Progress Publishers.

Minsky, H. (1975). *John Maynard Keynes*. New York: Columbia University Press.

Minsky, H. (1980). "Money, financial markets, and the coherence of a market economy", *Journal of Post Keynesian Economics*, 3 (1), 21–31.

Minsky, H. (1982). *Can "It" Happen Again? Essays on Instability and Finance*. Armonk: M.E. Sharpe.

Minsky, H. (1991). Finance crises: systemic or idiosyncratic. The Levy Economics Institute Working Paper 51, April.

Minsky, H. (1994). "Financial instability hypothesis", in P. Arestis and M. Sawyer (eds), *The Elgar Companion to Radical Political Economy*. Aldershot: Edward Elgar.

Morrison, G. (1967). *Liquidity Preference of Commercial Banks*. Chicago: University of Chicago Press.

Myrdal, G. (1965). *Monetary Equilibrium*. New York: Augustus M. Kelley.

Ohlin, B. (1937). "Rejoinder", *The Economic Journal*, 47 (187), 423–427.

Peden, G. C., ed. (2004). *Keynes and his Critics. Treasury Responses to the Keynesian Revolution 1925–1946*. Oxford: Oxford University Press for The British Academy.

Richardson, G. (2006). Bank distress during the great contraction, 1929 to 1933, new data from the archives of the Board of Governors, NBER Working Paper 12590.

Robertson, D. (1988). *Essays in Monetary Theory*. Westport: Hyperion Press.

Robinson, J. (1979). *The Generalization of The General Theory and Other Essays*. London: Macmillan.

Rymes, T. (1989). *Keynes's Lectures, 1932–35*. London: Macmillan for The Royal Economic Society.

Runde, J. (1994). "Keynesian uncertainty and liquidity preference", *Cambridge Journal of Economics*, 18 (2), 129–144.

Schumpeter, J. (2005). *Business Cycles. A Theoretical, Historical and Statistical Analysis of the Capitalist Process*. Chevy Chase: Bartleby's Books and Mansfield Centre: Martino Publishing.

Smithin, J. (2013). "Keynes's theories of money and banking in the Treatise and The General Theory", *Review of Keynesian Economics*, 1 (2), 242–256.

Sorkin, A. R. (2010). *Too Big to Fail: The Inside Story of How Wall Street and Washington Fought to Save the Financial System – and Themselves*. New York: Penguin Books.

Strahan, P. (2010). "Liquidity production in twenty-first-century banking", in A. Berger, P. Molyneux and J. Wilson (eds), *The Oxford Handbook of Banking*. Oxford: Oxford University Press.

Temin, P. (1976). *Did Monetary Forces Cause the Great Depression?*, New York: W. W. Norton.

Tobin, J. (1985). "Theoretical issues in macroeconomics", in G. Feiwell (ed.), *Issues in Contemporary Macroeconomics and Distribution*. London: Macmillan.

Tobin, J. (1987). *Essays in Economics. Volume 1: Macroeconomics*. Cambridge: The MIT Press.

Wattel, H., ed. (1985). *The Policy Consequences of John Maynard Keynes*. Armonk: M.E. Sharpe.

Weintraub, S. (1978). *Keynes, Keynesians and Monetarists*. Philadelphia: University of Pennsylvania Press.

Wicksell, K. (2007). *Lectures on Political Economy. Volume 2: Money*. Auburn: Ludwig von Mises Institute.

Wilson, T. (1982). "Policy in war and peace: the recommendations of J. M. Keynes", in A. P. Thirwall (ed.), *Keynes as Policy Adviser*. London: Macmillan.

Index

For Product Safety Concerns and Information please contact our EU
representative GPSR@taylorandfrancis.com Taylor & Francis Verlag GmbH,
Kaufingerstraße 24, 80331 München, Germany

Printed and bound by CPI Group (UK) Ltd, Croydon, CR0 4YY
08/05/2025
01864329-0003